Producing, Preparing, Exhibiting, & Judging Bee Produce.

ILLUSTRATED.

By WILLIAM HERROD, F.E.S.

Copyright © 2013 Read Books Ltd.
This book is copyright and may not be
reproduced or copied in any way without
the express permission of the publisher in writing

British Library Cataloguing-in-Publication Data
A catalogue record for this book is available from the
British Library

Bee Keeping

Beekeeping (or apiculture, from Latin: *apis* 'bee') is quite simply, the maintenance of honey bee colonies. A beekeeper (or apiarist) keeps bees in order to collect their honey and other products that the hive produces (including beeswax, propolis, pollen, and royal jelly), to pollinate crops, or to produce bees for sale to other beekeepers. A location where bees are kept is called an apiary or 'bee yard.' Depictions of humans collecting honey from wild bees date to 15,000 years ago, and efforts to domesticate them are shown in Egyptian art around 4,500 years ago. Simple hives and smoke were used and honey was stored in jars, some of which were found in the tombs of pharaohs such as Tutankhamun.

The beginnings of 'bee domestication' are uncertain, however early evidence points to the use of hives made of hollow logs, wooden boxes, pottery vessels and woven straw baskets. On the walls of the sun temple of Nyuserre Ini (an ancient Egyptian Pharo) from the Fifth Dynasty, 2422 BCE, workers are depicted blowing smoke into hives as they are removing honeycombs. Inscriptions detailing the production of honey have also been found on the tomb of Pabasa (an Egyptian nobleman) from the Twenty-sixth Dynasty (c. 650 BCE), depicting pouring honey in jars and cylindrical hives. Amazingly though, archaeological finds relating to beekeeping have been discovered at Rehov, a Bronze and Iron Age archaeological site in the Jordan Valley, Israel.

Thirty intact hives, made of straw and unbaked clay, were discovered in the ruins of the city, dating from about 900 BCE. The hives were found in orderly rows, three high, in a manner that could have accommodated around 100 hives, held more than 1 million bees and had a potential annual yield of 500 kilograms of honey and 70 kilograms of beeswax!

It wasn't until the eighteenth century that European understanding of the colonies and biology of bees allowed the construction of the moveable comb hive so that honey could be harvested without destroying the entire colony. In this 'Enlightenment' period, natural philosophers undertook the scientific study of bee colonies and began to understand the complex and hidden world of bee biology. Preeminent among these scientific pioneers were Swammerdam, René Antoine Ferchault de Réaumur, Charles Bonnet and the Swiss scientist Francois Huber. Huber was the most prolific however, regarded as 'the father of modern bee science', and was the first man to prove by observation and experiment that queens are physically inseminated by drones outside the confines of hives, usually a great distance away. Huber built improved glass-walled observation hives and sectional hives that could be opened like the leaves of a book. This allowed inspecting individual wax combs and greatly improved direct observation of hive activity. Although he went blind before he was twenty, Huber employed a secretary, Francois Burnens, to make daily observations, conduct careful experiments, and keep accurate notes for more than twenty years.

Early forms of honey collecting entailed the destruction of the entire colony when the honey was harvested. The wild hive was crudely broken into, using smoke to suppress the bees, the honeycombs were torn out and smashed up — along with the eggs, larvae and honey they contained. The liquid honey from the destroyed brood nest was strained through a sieve or basket. This was destructive and unhygienic, but for hunter-gatherer societies this did not matter, since the honey was generally consumed immediately and there were always more wild colonies to exploit. It took until the nineteenth century to revolutionise this aspect of beekeeping practice – when the American, Lorenzo Lorraine Langstroth made practical use of Huber's earlier discovery that there was a specific spatial measurement between the wax combs, later called *the bee space*, which bees do not block with wax, but keep as a free passage. Having determined this bee space (between 5 and 8 mm, or 1/4 to 3/8"), Langstroth then designed a series of wooden frames within a rectangular hive box, carefully maintaining the correct space between successive frames, and found that the bees would build parallel honeycombs in the box without bonding them to each other or to the hive walls.

Modern day beekeeping has remained relatively unchanged. In terms of keeping practice, the first line of protection and care – is always sound knowledge. Beekeepers are usually well versed in the relevant information; biology, behaviour, nutrition - and also wear protective clothing. Novice beekeepers commonly wear gloves and a hooded suit or hat and veil, but some experienced beekeepers elect not to use gloves because they inhibit delicate manipulations. The face and neck are the most important areas to protect (as a sting here will lead to much more pain and swelling than a sting elsewhere), so most beekeepers wear at least a veil. As an interesting note, protective clothing is generally white, and of a smooth material. This is because it provides the maximum differentiation from the colony's natural predators (bears, skunks, etc.), which tend to be dark-coloured and furry. Most beekeepers also use a 'smoker'—a device designed to generate smoke from the incomplete combustion of various fuels. Smoke calms bees; it initiates a feeding response in anticipation of possible hive abandonment due to fire. Smoke also masks alarm pheromones released by guard bees or when bees are squashed in an inspection. The ensuing confusion creates an opportunity for the beekeeper to open the hive and work without triggering a defensive reaction.

Such practices are generally associated with rural locations, and traditional farming endeavours. However, more recently, urban beekeeping has emerged; an attempt to revert to a less industrialized way of obtaining honey by utilizing small-scale colonies that pollinate urban gardens. Urban apiculture has undergone a renaissance in the first decade of the twenty-first century, and urban beekeeping is seen by many as a growing trend; it has recently been legalized in cities where it was previously banned. Paris, Berlin, London, Tokyo, Melbourne and Washington DC are among beekeeping cities. Some have found that 'city bees' are actually healthier than 'rural bees' because there are fewer pesticides and greater biodiversity. Urban bees may fail to find forage, however, and homeowners can use their landscapes to help feed local bee populations by planting flowers that provide nectar and pollen. As is evident from this short introduction, 'Bee-Keeping' is an incredibly ancient practice. We hope the current reader is inspired by this book to be more 'bee aware', whether that's via planting appropriate flowers, keeping bees or merely appreciating! Enjoy.

Dedicated to

MY PARENTS

to whose careful training and wise counsels I attribute my success in life.

PREFACE.

By Thos. William Cowan, F.L.S., F.G.S., etc.

I have been asked to write a short preface for this book, and I do so with pleasure, as it is a book that supplies a long-felt want. The chapters are written by one who not only has a complete grasp of the subject on which it treats, but who from long practical experience is especially qualified for the task. No one has had better opportunities of studying the question, for Mr. Herrod has had more experience in managing the largest and most important shows in the country than any one, and in this book we have the practical results of his experience clearly stated for the benefit of those desiring to produce and prepare exhibits with some expectation of gaining prizes. In addition to the advice for the producer, there are useful hints as to judges and judging. Sometimes complaints are made about the judging at shows, and it is very important that properly qualified persons should be appointed. Those aspiring to such qualification will do well to study the advice given. Some judges have fads which they insist upon, but a good judge will take a broad view of the matter and lay aside any particular fad he may cherish. I recollect when I first showed some supers of honey at the Crystal Palace show in 1874, the judges admitted that they were among the finest of any in the show, but disqualified them because the glass frames that were put on them were screwed down to prevent visitors from tampering with the combs. There were only two screws in each, and it would have been easy to remove them, but instead of doing this the exhibits were disqualified, much to everyone's astonishment. Although

PREFACE.

there was no rule in the schedule prohibiting the protection of exhibits in this way, I made no protest, but learnt the lesson, and made up my mind never to be so narrow, should I be called upon at any time to judge.

This book will be especially useful to those having the management of shows, and it fills a gap in bee literature that has long existed. In these days when books appear like mushrooms, and when every one who has a smattering of bee-keeping thinks he must compile a book, and in doing so liberally cribs from other writings, it is refreshing to find that this one is entirely original, written from practical experience, and contains the most valuable information on the subject. If the simple directions given are faithfully carried out, exhibiting must result in not only a source of pleasure, but also of profit to the bee-keeper.

CONTENTS.

CHAP. PAGE.
I.—Introduction 1
II.—The Judge—The Exhibitor—Duties of Secretaries and Stewards 5
III.—Advice to Exhibitors—Advantages and Inducements of Exhibiting 19
IV.—Points to be Observed, and Methods of Judging ... 34
V.—Judging by Points 50
VI.—Producing and Preparing Extracted Honey ... 55
VII.—Producing and Preparing Comb Honey 67
VIII.—Producing and Preparing Wax 83
IX.—Producing and Preparing Bye-Products, with Recipes 91
X.—Observatory Hives, Appliances, Trophies, and Scientific Exhibits 105
XI.—Packing Exhibits 122
XII.—Despatching Exhibits 135
XIII.—Showing as a Means of Disposing of Honey ... 141
XIV.—Rules, Regulations, and Schedules 144
XV.—Attractive and Educational Work 153
Index 167

LIST OF ILLUSTRATIONS.

	PAGE.
Address Label	136
Appliance Classes, Lincolnshire Show	48
Australian Exhibit (Queensland)	72
Back of Post Card, Ruled and Filled for Results	137
Badly-constructed Travelling Crate	129
Badly Packed Box, with 15 Screws	125
Badly Packed Jars	124
Badly Packed Sections	129
Badly-staged Shop Window Display	116
Bee Showing Wax Scales	83
Bell Glass Super	79
Box Travelling Crate for Sections	130
Brown, Mr. R.	13
Cake Cut for Judging	46
Cardboard Cases for Jars	123
Cardboard Show Cases	77
Challenge Cup and Pendant (Notts)	33
Class of Medium Honey (Grocers)	28
Class of Sections (Grocers)	69
Coronation Challenge Cup (B.B.K.A.)	31
County Honey Trophies (South Kensington)	25
County Honey Trophy (Berks)	102
County Honey Trophy (Hunts)	103
County Honey Trophy (Lancs., South Kensington)	117
County Honey Trophy (Notts)	63
Cowan and Carr, Messrs., Judging	6
Crawshaw, Mr. L. S.	9
Cumbersome Demonstrating Tent	158
Dant, Mr. E. F.	17
Dell, Mr. A. S.	17
Demonstrating Tent, Packed	155
Display of Prize Heather Honey by Lipton	40
Dyer, Mr. C. W.	18
Eales, Mr. C. L. M.	13
Exhibit of Granulated Honey (Spoilt by Tasting)	16
Exhibit of Honey Products	100
Exhibits of Wax not Properly Staged (Retail Class)	90

LIST OF ILLUSTRATIONS (*Continued*).

	PAGE.
Exhibits of Wax (Retail Class)	89
Exhibits Packed for Return (Grocers)	133
Faked Sections	42
Glazed Section (Full Width and Cut Down)	74
Gold, Silver, and Bronze Medals Won by Author	36
Group of Noted Bee-keepers	26
Hayes, Mr. G.	12
Heather Honey Press	65
Herrod, Mr. J.	11
"Herrod" Demonstrating Tent in Use	156
"Herrod" Skep Carrier	161
Hertford Association Show	37
Honey-comb Design	80
Honey-comb Design	81
Honey Competition (Grocers, Newcastle)	94
Honey Exhibits at Royal Show (Norwich)	96
Honey Exhibits (Dairy Show)	35
Honey Pavilion (Zurich Exhibition)	2
Honey Sale Stall	142
Home-made Observatory Hive	118
Home-made Hive	119
Home-made Solar Extractor	120
How Not to Exhibit Sections	77
How Not to Stage a Trophy	112
Indoor Demonstration by the Author	164
Indoor Demonstration Department (Grocers)	165
Japanese Honey Jar	47
Jar of Honey Packed for Post	132
Judging (D.M.M. and Mr. Crawshaw)	60
Lecturer's Demonstrating Table	157
Lecturer's Kit Packed on Small Motor Car	163
Macdonald, Mr. D. M. (D.M.M.)	8
Making Show Cases for Sections	73
Manufacturers' Exhibit	154
Method of Skewering Combs	160
Medals and Pendants (B.B.K.A.)	27
Method of Straining Wax	88
Method of Using Reid Taster	39
Mould of Wax Standing in Water	87
Monster Display of Honey in a London Shop Window	92
Non-competitive Exhibit (Mr. Allen)	51
Non-competitive Exhibit (R. H. Baynes and Co.)	29
Noted Prize-winners (Mr. and Mrs. Pearman)	52
Not the Way to Mould Wax	85
Noted Prize-winners (Mr. and Mrs. A. W. Weatherhogg)	55
Old-fashioned Geared Extractor	56

LIST OF ILLUSTRATIONS (*Continued*).

	PAGE.
Old-fashioned Super of Comb Honey	64
Old-fashioned Observatory Hive	3
Outdoor Lecture by the Author	98
Over Laced and Properly Laced Sections	75
Packed Sections (Side View)	128
Patchett, Mr. W.	15
Pendants (County Association)	32
Prize Cards (B.B.K.A.)	30
Prize Shallow Combs	44
Prize-winning Sections (Mr. Weatherhogg's)	41
Pugh, Mr. A. G.	10
Record Shallow Comb Class (Grocers)	45
"Reid" Honey Taster	38
Reid, Mr. W. F.	7
Record Class of Light Extracted Honey (Grocers)	53
Result of Bad Packing of Sections	128
Running Honey into Jars	58
Section Glazing Machine	76
Sections Packed in Non-returnable Box	127
Section Rack	68
Shop Window Display at Bedford	21
Show Case for Shallow Combs	78
Single Comb Observatory Hive	105
Template for Lace Edging on Sections	43
Three-Comb Observatory Hive	106
Travelling Box for Demonstration of Bees	162
Travelling Box for Jars	122
Travelling Crate for Sections	126
Trophy and Wax Exhibits	20
Trophy with Honey Products	110
Two-way Section	67
Ventilating a Supered Hive	70
Wax Properly Moulded and Protected	86
Walker, Mr. F.	7
Well-staged Shop Window Display	113
Well-staged Shop Window Display	114
Well-staged Trophy of Honey	108
Well-staged Trophy of Honey	109
Weston Solar Extractor	84
Woodley, Mr. W.	14
Wrong Method of Packing	131

CHAPTER I.

Introduction.

During the past thirty years the exhibiting of honey, wax, and their products has gradually increased, until at the present time it forms no inconsiderable part of the work of the bee-keeper. Although of such importance, it is a curious fact that up to the present no book has been written dealing with this branch of apiculture, consequently the requirements and methods pursued for the arrangement of shows and the preparation of exhibits for the show bench have only been obtainable by the practical experience of those interested. This of course has meant a great deal of expense and fruitless labour on the part of the exhibitor, for in the initial stage he was, as it were, groping in the dark.

During all my life I have had the unique experience, and good fortune, of coming in constant contact with the best judges and exhibitors of the day. My work has also been of such a nature that I have had the arranging and management of shows, from the smallest to the largest in the country, working my way up from the lowest position of the often reviled third class expert to the much coveted honour of judge. Therefore the knowledge that I possess has been gained by practice, and is not theoretical. I also pay grateful tribute to the great help and advice given me ungrudgingly at all times by those two veterans of the craft Mr. T. W. Cowan and the late Mr. W. Broughton Carr. No pupil could have had better tutors, and it is my sincere hope that I may continue to be the pupil of the former for many years to come.

Honey Pavilion, Zurich Exhibition, Nov. 1st, 1883.

I have frequently been asked, for many years past, to put my knowledge of this branch of work into book form, and in the following pages my endeavour has been to do this in as simple a manner as possible.

Although I hoped to complete and publish this book about eighteen months ago, circumstances arose which prevented me from carrying out that intention, and I must apologise to those who were led to expect it sooner. The delay, however, has not been without its advantages, for it has enabled me to include several items which would otherwise have been omitted.

For simplicity, and to make the book more interesting,

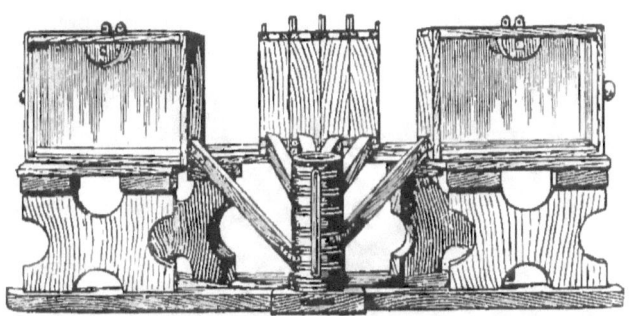

An Old-fashioned bservatory Hive, 1877.

I have introduced a large number of illustrations, most of which are from photographs, taken by myself, of actual exhibits and operations. I have neither written nor illustrated anything which I have not proved by practice to be sound, nor have I attempted to foist upon bee-keepers as my own work matter copied from other authors, which has unfortunately been the practice of some writers on bee-keeping.

For the loan of photographs and assistance in other ways I gratefully acknowledge my indebtedness to the following: Mr. T. W. Cowan, Mr. D. M. Macdonald, Mr. A. S. Dell, Mr. J. Benson, Sir Thomas Lipton, Mr. A. W. Weatherhogg,

Mr. F. J. Cribb, the Editor of "Farm Life," Mr. R. Allen, Mr. G. Hayes, the Editor of "The Chemist and Druggist," Mr. F. C. Kelley, Mr. G. Barnes, Mr. G. W. Judge, Mr. W. Dixon, Mr. A. Dewey, Messrs. Abbott Bros., Mr. W. P. Meadows, Mr. L. S. Crawshaw, Mr. J. Pearman, Mr. E. F. Dant, and Mr. G. Bush.

In conclusion, I may say that neither time, trouble, nor expense has been spared in the compilation of this work, in the hope that it will supply a long felt want, and, while being the means of increasing the number of exhibitors at our shows, will enable those who have already embarked upon the fascinating work of exhibiting to be more successful in future.

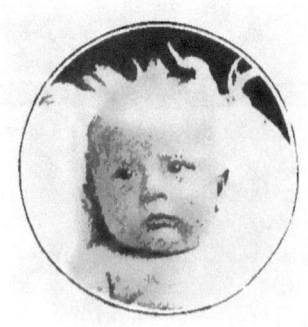

CHAPTER II.

The Judge—The Exhibitor—Duties of Secretaries and Stewards.

The Judge.

No doubt the complaint sometimes made by exhibitors of the incompetency of some judges is well founded. The judge should be a man above suspicion, not given to fads, very observant, and having a delicate palate. Above all, he should have been a successful bee-keeper and exhibitor himself. It is only by such experience that a thorough practical knowledge of the work can be obtained, theory in judging not being needed. Yet how often do we see judges appointed who have never even staged an exhibit, let alone taken a prize, and not infrequently such as have only kept bees a few years. No wonder that prizes have been awarded to syrup fed sections, others with one in a lot of twelve sealed only on one side, adulterated beeswax, observatory hives with no queen or the brood badly diseased. This is no fancy picture, for such cases are on record.

Judges are not born, nor are they made theoretically, but must serve an apprenticeship to obtain the necessary qualifications for this much coveted and responsible position.

When an exhibitor at flower shows, the writer was much annoyed at the judges of the horticultural section being asked to judge the honey. As a rule they knew as much about judging honey as he would have done about cucumbers. No matter how small the show may be, a properly qualified judge should be obtained.

This photograph is unique; it shows two of the most noted judges of modern times, Mr. T. W. Cowan and Mr. W. Broughton Carr. Though closely connected for twenty years, it was the first and last time they judged together. It was taken by the author at the Dairy Show, 1908 a few months before the death of Mr. Carr.

A Prominent Judge, Mr. W. F. Reid, F.I.C., F.C.S.

The judge must be painstaking, ever on the look-out for faking, and not afraid of spending time over his work.

A Well-known Judge, Mr. E. Walker.

8   *PRODUCING, PREPARING, EXHIBITING*

This statement may seem unnecessary, but a judge has been known to adjudicate on the whole of the exhibits at such an important show as that of the British Dairy Farmers' Association in less than half an hour. This happened some years ago, and it is needless to say he has never

A Noted Scotch Judge, Mr. D. M. Macdonald (D.M.M.).

been called upon to act in this capacity since that time. He never tasted a single sample, but judged by appearance only, and tested the density of the honey by the out-of-date method of inverting the bottle. On the other hand, the late Mr. T. J. Weston was an exemplary judge of honey, being possessed of a most delicate palate, and he has been known to replace, by taste only, six exhibits of extracted honey in their original order, after they had been mixed up.

We have some splendid judges at the present time, but it is a pity that they have not more time at their disposal to give to the work. No man is infallible, and though he may do his best, mistakes will occasionally occur. The exhibitor must therefore be forbearing and make due allowance. The fact that judges generally give their

A Northern Judge, Mr. L. S. Crawshaw.

services gratuitously, often at great inconvenience to themselves, must not be lost sight of. "More power to their tongue say we."

The Exhibitor.

Generally he is a right good fellow, ready and willing to help his competitors, especially the novice, with both labour and advice. It is easy to criticise the work of the judge, but the exhibitor must remember that he views his

10 PRODUCING, PREPARING, EXHIBITING

own exhibit from a biased standpoint, while the judge is unbiased and judges it by merit only. It is also most unkind and inconsiderate to badger the judge to give reasons for his various awards. A wise judge will refuse to argue with such unreasonable exhibitors.

Those really seeking information for their benefit and

A Judge and Exhibitor, Mr. A. G. Pugh.

further guidance the judge is always ready and willing to advise. The exhibitor should take defeat in the right spirit, with a resolve to profit by the experience, to persevere and do better in the future, instead of grumbling at the judge when the fault of non-success is either through his own ignorance of what is required or his ill-luck with the bees.

He should be forbearing to the secretary and steward of the show, and always ready to give a helping hand in staging or re-packing exhibits. Both of these officials do a great deal of hard and monotonous work of which the exhibitor knows nothing.

Secretaries and Stewards.

Very often the labour of the judge is added to considerably for want of thought and method. The schedule

Mr. J. Herrod, Judge, Exhibitor, and Demonstrator.

should be drawn up in such a manner that nothing remains doubtful; every condition should be clearly stated and not left to the discretion of the judge. Unless this is done, constant trouble will be experienced with the change of judges each year. The classes and exhibits should be arranged so as to avoid a muddle and in such a manner that the work may go on uninterruptedly without having to dodge about and thus probably missing some of the exhibits.

A judging book, properly arranged with the numbers written in, together with a copy of the schedule and regulations, should be placed in the judge's hands before he commences work. It is even better to send these by post, if possible, a few days before the show so that he may read over the rules and digest them while travelling, and thus save time.

A Judge, Exhibitor, and Demonstrator, Mr. G. Hayes.

Fix the time when the judging is to commence, insist upon everything being ready by that time, and avoid keeping the judge waiting for an hour or two, which is no rare occurrence at some shows. A judge's time is valuable; he should therefore know exactly when and where to arrive, and at what time he can get away, or other appointments and arrangements which he may have made will be

A Royal Show Judge, Mr. C. L. M. Eales.

The Well-known Exhibitor and Judge, Mr. R. Brown.

14 PRODUCING, PREPARING, EXHIBITING

The Veteran Exhibitor, Mr. Wm. Woodley, well known as the most successful Exhibitor of Sections.

seriously interfered with. Keeping to time also avoids the impatience often shown by the public when kept waiting

AND JUDGING BEE PRODUCE. 15

to view the exhibits beyond the hour stated for the opening of the show. The steward should see that all the exhibits conform to the rules and regulations, and, if they do not, point out the disqualifications to the judge. Scales for weighing wax should be secured. Water should be provided for washing the hands, and also a towel for drying them.

A Noted Lincolnshire Prize Winner, Mr. W. Patchett.

for honey sticks tenaciously, making one uncomfortable as well as spoiling clothes. Soda water, dry biscuits, or apples should also be provided, so that the sensitiveness of the judge's palate may be retained right through his work. It should not be forgotten that he cannot live upon honey alone, therefore provide him at the proper time with lunch. To avoid trouble and annoyance, an entrance ticket should be despatched to him by post a day or two before the show. Badges should always be provided, as they are treasured by many judges as mementos of their work, and, as a rule, are practically the only compensation they receive for their labour.

A careful supervision of the exhibits should be provided against the general public, who should not be allowed to touch, open, or taste exhibits indiscriminately. I have seen jars in exhibits at some shows half emptied by the continual tasting by visitors. An exhibit of granulated honey spoiled in this way is shown at Fig. 1. The staging for

Fig. 1. Exhibit of Granulated Honey spoilt by visitors tasting.

jars and sections should be on the step principle. This makes a more imposing show, and enables the judge to carry out his work with greater expedition than when the exhibits are staged on a flat table. No one but the steward and secretary should be present while the judge is carrying out his work. This will facilitate matters, and his attention will not be distracted from his work, which would be the case if a number of people were standing about or passing round. If two judges are at work it is inconvenient for them to carry on verbal criticisms with an audience surrounding

Mr. A. S. Dell, one of the most successful Exhibitors of Honey and Honey Products.

A Prominent Prize Winner, Mr. E. F. Dant of R. H. Baynes & Co.

18   BEE PRODUCE.

A Successful Exhibitor, Mr. C. W. Dyer.

them, amongst whom there might be an exhibitor foolish enough to try and argue with them on an adverse criticism of his own exhibit. No secretaries or stewards should ever be exhibitors at a show which they are controlling.

CHAPTER III.

Advice to Exhibitors.

Advantages and Inducements of Exhibiting.

Exhibitors should first read over the rules of each show at which they intend to exhibit carefully. It should not be taken for granted that the regulations governing one show apply to all. This is by no means the case, for it will be found that they vary considerably. Regulations are revised each year and alterations are made at most shows. I have often seen exhibitors lose prizes through carelessness in this respect. A technical error may cause the disqualification of exhibits that might otherwise have won a prize.

It is advisable, even absolutely necessary, for exhibitors to visit shows from time to time to compare their exhibits with those of others as well as to pick up information and wrinkles. A few shillings spent in this way is a good investment, for by seeing what is actually required many pounds may be saved in useless entry fees and railway carriage on exhibits which would not stand the shadow of a chance of winning prizes. The following are a few of the mistakes made by exhibitors : (1) Honey is shown in the wrong class according to colour. This can be avoided by obtaining and using the British Bee-keepers' Association's two grading glasses, supplied by "The British Bee Journal," the instructions for using which are as follows :
" *One* piece of glass supplied herewith when held up to ordinary daylight—not sunlight—shows the *lightest* shade allowable, and the *two* pieces in juxtaposition denote the *darkest* shade permitted in classes for Medium Coloured Extracted Honey. The test of colour must be made with honey in the bottles in which it is to be exhibited, and in *no other way.*"

Trophy and Wax Exhibits, Grocers' Exhibition at the Agricultural Hall, London, 1910.

Fig. 2. R. Brown & Son's Winning Exhibit, Royal Show, Norwich, 1911, shown in shop of its purchaser at Bedford.

(2) Granulated honey is shown in the class intended for liquid honey. (3) Trade or association labels are put on the jars or sections when the rule distinctly states that this must not be done. (4) No numbers put on, or other number labels used instead of those supplied by the secretary. (5) Trophies larger than the dimensions specified in the schedule or a greater or less weight of honey than is allowed. (6) Jars too tall. (7) Heather blend shown in classes where it is distinctly stated that the honey must be "other than heather." (8) Six jars or sections sent instead of twelve. (9) Sections sent unglazed. (10) Insufficient weight of wax. (11) Sections overlaced. (12) Exhibits all packed in one box instead of in separate boxes. (13) Tall sections shown instead of the ordinary $4\frac{1}{4}$ by $4\frac{3}{4}$in. (14) A great mistake is repeatedly made in placing number labels on the caps of jars. They do not stick to metal but come off very quickly, and thus cause confusion if the jars are moved by the judges. The numbers should always be placed on the side of a jar, about one inch from the bottom.

Advantages of Exhibiting.

Undoubtedly the show bench is one of the best means of creating a market for the produce of the apiary. This is very clearly illustrated by the keenness of trade customers to purchase prize exhibits at the large shows, more especially the trophies in their entirety, and if the premier honour is won almost any price can be obtained. Fig. 2 shows the first prize trophy of Messrs. R. Brown and Son, of Somersham, at the Royal Show, held at Norwich in 1911, staged in the window of its purchaser, Tunks and Tisdall, Ltd., dairymen, Bedford. This also applies to other classes, and it is not unusual for first prize exhibits to realise as much as fifteen shillings per dozen. At local shows obtaining a prize means a quick disposal of all the produce at more remunerative prices than would otherwise be the case, and results in securing regular customers. We have such customers to-day who were obtained in this

AND JUDGING BEE PRODUCE.

manner many years ago. It is an established fact that the sale classes at the Grocers and Confectioners' Exhibitions have been the means of disposing of many tons of honey. A show is also a good means of educating consumers respecting the various forms and qualities in which honey can be obtained, its various domestic uses as a sweetening agent in cakes and all kinds of confectionery, and its medicinal virtues. It also shows the superiority of the produce of the British Islands over that of other countries. In recent foreign publications the large honey shows held in this country were referred to as examples of what can and should be done for bee-keepers in this way, and they were urging their own associations to work on similar lines, which is a great compliment to us.

COMPLIMENTARY TICKET. . . .

EXHIBITION
OF

Bees, Honey and Honey Products
Will be held at

11, RAILWAY ROAD, LEIGH,

From October 21st to November 6th inclusive.
Open daily from 3 p.m.

That even a private exhibition is profitable, not only to the bee-keeper but also for charitable objects, is clearly shown by the experience of that noted exhibitor A. S. Dell, who arranged one in his own town and kept it going for three weeks. Complimentary tickets were sent out, a large amount of advertising by posters was done, and frequent lectures were given during each day, the result being a great success, not only for the exhibitor, but also the infirmary to which the proceeds were given. Here is a reproduction of the complimentary ticket and the programme, which is got up very artistically.

DESCRIPTIVE CATALOGUE

OF THE VARIOUS EXHIBITS.

1. Trophy of Honey obtained from FRUIT TREE BLOSSOM.
2. Trophy of Honey obtained from WHITE CLOVER.
3. Trophy of Honey obtained from SAINFOIN.
4. Trophy of Honey obtained from CLOVER AND HEATHER.
5. Trophy of Honey obtained from HEATHER.
6. Trophy of Honey obtained from CLOVER, SAINFOIN AND HEATHER, weighing upwards of 1500 lbs. net.
7. Trophy of Honey, facsimile of which was awarded the Royal Lancashire Cup (4 times).
8. BEESWAX.
9. OBSERVATORY HIVE WITH BEES.
10. ANCIENT AND MODERN HIVES.
11. Machine used for extracting Honey from the Comb.
12. 3 Challenge Cups, Numerous Silver and Bronze Medals awarded in 1909.

"Come, feast thine eyes on Nature's Finest Food!"

Bees, Honey & Honey Products

EXHIBITION

Will be held at

11. RAILWAY ROAD, LEIGH,

From Oct. 21st to Nov. 6th inclusive.
Open daily from 3-0 p.m.

Showing Bees in Observatory Hives. Upwards of 3,000 lbs. of Honey.

The Largest Exhibition ever held by any individual Bee-keeper in England.

All the Exhibits will be FULLY EXPLAINED

ADMISSION BY CATALOGUE.

The Proceeds from which will be given to the Leigh Infirmary.

A. S. DELL,
The County Apiaries, Leigh.

County Honey Trophies at The British Bee-Keepers' Association Show at the Indian and Colonial Exhibition, South Kensington, July 30th, 1886.

PRODUCING, PREPARING, EXHIBITING

Inducements to Exhibit.

There are many, and probably the first consideration of the majority would be the "prize-money." There is, however, also the social side of the question to be considered. By visiting shows, bee-keepers are brought into touch with each other, so that, instead of a paper acquaintance, a personal one is made. This has oft-times resulted in a life-long friendship and correspondence. How interesting and pleasant it is, after the work of staging is over, to get together, have a friendly chat, and compare notes of success or failure. It broadens one's outlook on life, makes

A Group of Noted Bee-keepers waiting for the Judges' Awards of County Honey Trophy, Royal Show, Manchester, June 23rd, 1897.

us realise that others have their failures and disappointments as well as their successes, and gives us encouragement to persevere. It is also a healthy recreation, for, instead of remaining at home from one year's end to the other, as many would do, always among the same surroundings, with no relaxation from the regular routine work, we are taken to fresh scenes, which, with a little excitement added, enable us to return home rested and refreshed to continue our work with renewed vigour.

At many shows it is also possible to win cups and medals. These are a great inducement to a large number of

AND JUDGING BEE PRODUCE.

exhibitors, who have frequently told me that they would far rather win a cup or medal than money prizes. Associations affiliated to The British Bee-keepers' Association have the privilege of obtaining one silver and one bronze medal or pendant for competition each year by their members. The medals are substantial and pretty, as will

Fig. 3. Medals and Pendants of the British Bee-Keepers' Association.

be seen by Fig. 3, but apart from the honour of winning them, they are well worth possessing. I well remember how proud I was of the first one I won. If the exhibitor does not desire the large medal, a neat pendant suitable for a watch chain may be had in its place. This is also of a very neat design, as will be seen in Fig. 3. Cards of beautiful design with an embossed copy of the medals in natural colours have been provided at great expense by the British

The largest class of Medium Extracted Honey ever shown in this country. Forty-seven exhibits (564 jars), on staging fifty feet long. Grocers' Exhibition at the Agricultural Hall, London, 1911.

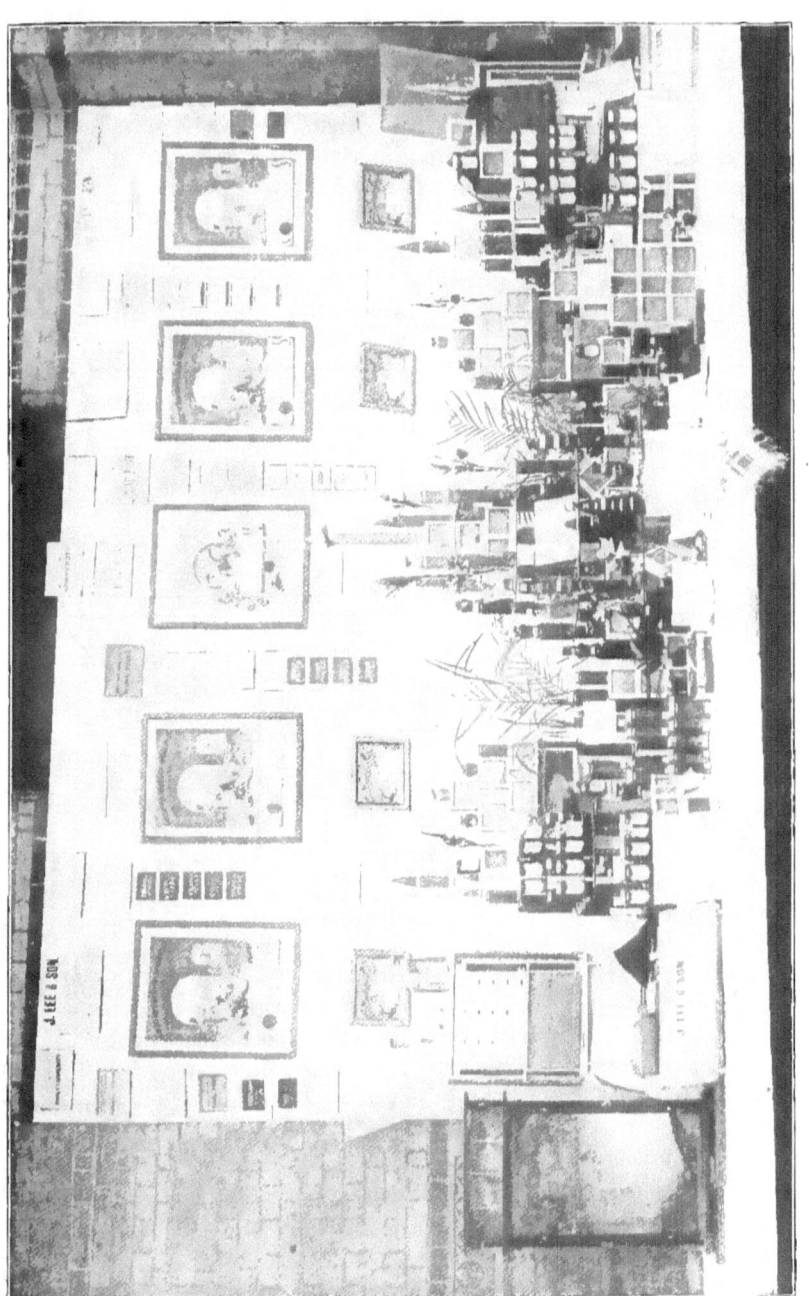

A Fine Non-competitive Exhibit by R. H. Baynes & Co., Cambridge. Note the prize cards.

Bee-keepers' Association with which the exhibitor can decorate his winning exhibits during the show. (Fig. 4.) Silver cups are lasting mementos of honours won. The parent association offered a Coronation Challenge Cup valued at twenty-five guineas at the Dairy Show in 1902. This was to be won three times before it became the absolute property of the winner. It was won for the third time in

Fig. 4. Prize Cards of the British Bee-Keepers' Association.

1906 by Mr. H. W. Seymour, of Henley-on-Thames, who was in those days a prominent exhibitor and prize-winner.

A glance at Fig. 5 will show that the prize was worthy of the effort to gain it. This cup has been taken away by him to his new home in Australia, and will undoubtedly remind him of the close link which binds him to the old country.

Very often County Associations have pendants of their own, several being as a rule offered as prizes at the annual show. Fig. 6 shows the pendants of the Notts., Lincs., and Lancs. Associations.

Fig. 5. The British Bee-Keepers' Association's Coronation Challenge Cup. Value twenty-five guineas.

32 BEE PRODUCE.

Silver cups are also sometimes offered. The Challenge Cup of the Nottinghamshire Bee-keepers' Association is shown at Fig. 7, with the silver pendant, one of which is presented to the winner each year.

Fig. 6. Pendants of Lancs., Lincs., and Notts. Associations.

Unlike a great many other pursuits where exhibiting is confined to the moneyed classes, the exhibition of bee produce and the winning of prizes is open to the person who can only afford a few hives as well as to those who have a large number. In both cases the bees work upon the same flowers without let or hindrance. There is no monopoly, for the person with a few hives stands just the same chance of winning prizes as the large apiarist, and more than once I have seen an exhibitor with only one hive carry off premier honours.

Fig. 7. The Challenge Cup and Pendant of the Notts. Association.

CHAPTER IV.

Points to be Observed, and Methods of Judging.

In judging honey the following points, taken in the order of their importance, are given.

Liquid.—Flavour, density, colour, aroma, brightness, and general get-up. Flavour is of paramount importance. If our food has no flavour we do not relish it. In deciding this much depends upon the individual taste of the judge. It should have a nice mellow, definite taste which would enable the judge to tell the source from which it was obtained, with the honey, as it were, rolling smoothly over the tongue and no burning or tickling sensation in the throat after it was swallowed. *Density.*—In all cases the honey should be as thick as possible, though this should not be allowed to over-rule flavour too much. *Colour.*—For light classes it should be a clear, bright amber. It is a mistake to imagine that to win a prize it is necessary for the honey to be water-white.

Often the lightest and thickest honey is absolutely devoid of either flavour or aroma; therefore, as the taste is the principal thing in our food, such exhibits would stand very little chance in competition with better flavoured honey.

Classes for medium and dark are defined by the colours stated. *Aroma.*—This should be delicate and distinctly perceptible so that the source from which the honey was obtained may be recognised. To fully appreciate aroma, the judge should remove the cap from the jar himself and immediately smell the honey. If the jars remain uncapped for some time much of the aroma will be dissipated.

Where heather is barred in the dark and medium classes, care is necessary, for often a slight mixture of

Honey Exhibits, Dairy Show, 1908, at the Agricultural Hall, London, with Sale Stalls in the distance.

hawthorn honey gives the impression that heather is present, and with only a slight mixture it is very difficult for even the most experienced to tell which it is. *Brightness.*—The honey in all three grades should be clear and bright. Dull and muddy exhibits have not a pleasing appearance and should be altogether discouraged. *General get-up.*—The honey should look as clean and neat as possible, and be contained in screw cap jars and not in what are called " tie-overs." It should, moreover, be quite free from bits of wax and other impurities.

A Few of the Gold, Silver, and Bronze Medals won by the Author.

It is necessary to watch for these very closely as the particles are often so minute that only a careful inspection will enable one to detect them. The presence of scum should be penalised very heavily. Preparation of extracted honey is dependent on the skill of the exhibitor, and if scum is allowed to remain it shows great neglect on his part.

Show of the Hertford, Ware, and District Association.

Granulated Honey.—This should be as white as possible, with a nice, smooth, even grain, and no sign of fermentation. Flavour similar to that required for liquid honey. There should be no flakiness, but the honey should be even and in contact with the jar all round.

Heather.—This should have a bitterish sweet taste, but not too pronounced, be of a rich dark amber colour, and have a gelatinous consistency. One peculiarity of heather honey is the fact that owing to its gelatinous nature the air bubbles which get in during the pressing process never

38 PRODUCING, PREPARING, EXHIBITING

rise, but give it a very nice appearance, and this is sometimes taken by the inexperienced as a sign of fermentation.

Heather Blend.—This should be prepared so that a delicate flavour of heather is noticeable, but it should not be too strong. The consistency must be similar to that of good clover honey.

The judge ought not to be led astray by first impressions but should carry out his duties thoroughly. In every case it is necessary that the honey should be tasted. For this purpose he must provide himself with a " Reid " honey-taster, Fig. 8. This is a small glass rod, rounded at one end for use with extracted honey, and with a small knob at the other for opening single cells in comb honey for tasting, and to avoid spoiling the appearance of the sections.

The taster can be used for testing the density by inserting it into the honey and withdrawing it sharply several times. This is much better than the old method of inverting the jar and watching the speed of the air bubble, which is an out-of-date method and unreliable, for if the jar is filled to the top the air bubble will be some time in starting, will travel slowly, and give a wrong impression of the density. For the purpose of tasting, a small portion of honey is taken on the rounded end of the taster by dipping it into the jar. It should then be transferred to the index finger as seen at Fig. 9, and from this to the mouth. This is much better than the detestable and objectionable, as well as from a hygienic point of view unclean practice, of dipping the taster into the honey and then placing it directly into the mouth, and so on from sample to sample, which is sometimes followed. Exhibits of granulated honey should not be spoiled by digging into them and tasting from every jar, as this discourages exhibitors. A sample from one jar is quite sufficient to judge of the remainder.

Fig. 8. " Reid " Honey-taster.

AND JUDGING BEE PRODUCE.

Colour can be ascertained by means of the grading glasses previously mentioned, with which full instructions for their use are issued.

Sections.—These should be judged by the colour of capping, which in clover is a brightish white, in sainfoin a pale straw colour, and in heather a dead white, with the honey opaque. It would be an advantage if separate classes could be arranged for sainfoin sections, as they are only obtainable

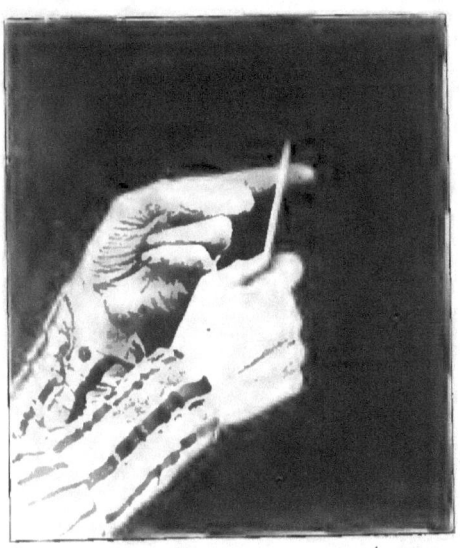

Fig. 9. The **Method of using the "Reid" Honey-taster.**

in certain districts with a chalk subsoil. Their attractiveness in the eyes of many of the judges places them in unfair competition with the white cappings of clover honey. All sections should be well and evenly filled, with an absence of pop-holes, and the cappings should be thin and not greasy-looking. For preference the comb should consist of worker cells, as this has a finer appearance.

Each exhibit should be tasted because appearances are sometimes deceptive, and what looks like a splendid sample

A Unique Display of Prize Heather Honey by Lipton, Ltd., Edinburgh.

Two Dozen Prize-winning Sections produced by Mr. A. W. Weatherhogg.

is often not only rank in flavour but tasteless or very thin. It is unfair to spoil an exhibit by digging right into the centre of a section with a spoon, which is the delight of some adjudicators. As recently as last season I came across a case where the judge insisted in cutting out each comb from the woodwork of the section to see that it was all right, and he served every section in each exhibit in the same way. Fortunately it was at a very small show, and there were not many sections he could mutilate in this way.

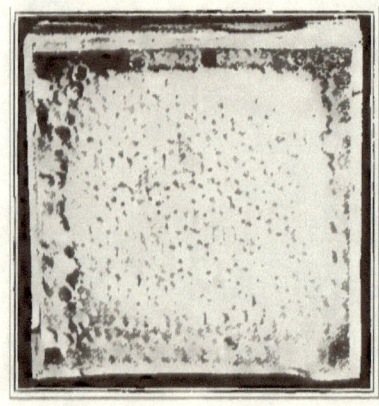 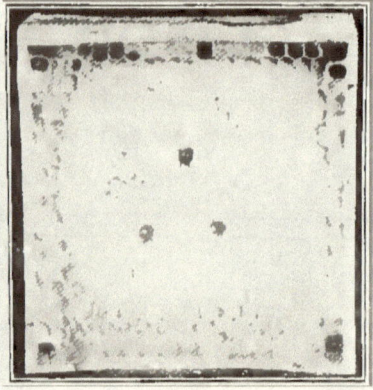

Fig. 10. Section faked by having cappings stuck on unsealed cells.   The same section with faked cappings removed.

By means of the specially made end of the " Reid " taster one cell only, and that at the side, need be opened and the honey tasted without doing any damage to the section.

The production of good sections depends quite as much on the bee-keeper as the bees, whose labour should not be destroyed in a wanton manner.

A sharp look-out should be kept for detecting granulation, also faking, i.e., placing loose cappings over odd cells that have not been sealed, see Fig. 10. This can only be done by a careful examination of both sides of each individual section, such inspection being especially necessary where the sections are staged against a wall or tent side. Sometimes sugar syrup feeding is resorted to by unscrupulous exhibitors. If sections have been made from syrup the cappings will appear dull and dead white, and the wax look unnatural. Tasting will at once reveal the source from which the contents were obtained. Overlacing is easily detected, but to be quite sure the judge should use a plate-glass template, Fig. 11, three-and-a-half inches square, and cut very accurately. A knob in the centre would make it more convenient to hold in position, and then all the edges could be seen at the same time.

Fig. 11. Template for lace edging on sections.

If the template is made of glass it is much easier to see if the lace paper is carried too far, as the edges will show through the glass. This cannot be done with an opaque one, nor can such accurate measurements be carried out with a rule.

Shallow Combs.—In these the comb should be perfectly straight but project beyond the woodwork sufficiently to enable it to be uncapped expeditiously. It must be free from the slightest sign of granulation, and should consist of drone comb, each cell clearly defined. Weight alone should not count.

Bell Glasses.—These should be clean and neat in appearance, with the honey of good colour and well sealed. The combs must be as regular as it is possible to get them.

Wax.—This should be pale, clear yellow, lemon or primrose colour, but if obtained from cappings only it is sometimes almost white. Extremes in colour should be avoided.

It should have a delicate aroma, be perfectly clean, without cracks or flaws. The plainer it is moulded the better. It must be free from adulteration and not bleached. When placed in the mouth and masticated it should not become of a pasty nature, nor yet adhere to the teeth, and be almost tasteless. It should break with a fine grained shell-like fracture. If bleached or adulterated these characteristics are absent. The most likely faults encountered are due to spoiling by overheating in the process of rendering or melting without water, an absence of aroma, insufficient cleaning leaving grit, dirt and honey in the wax, and sometimes adulteration.

Prize Shallow Combs.

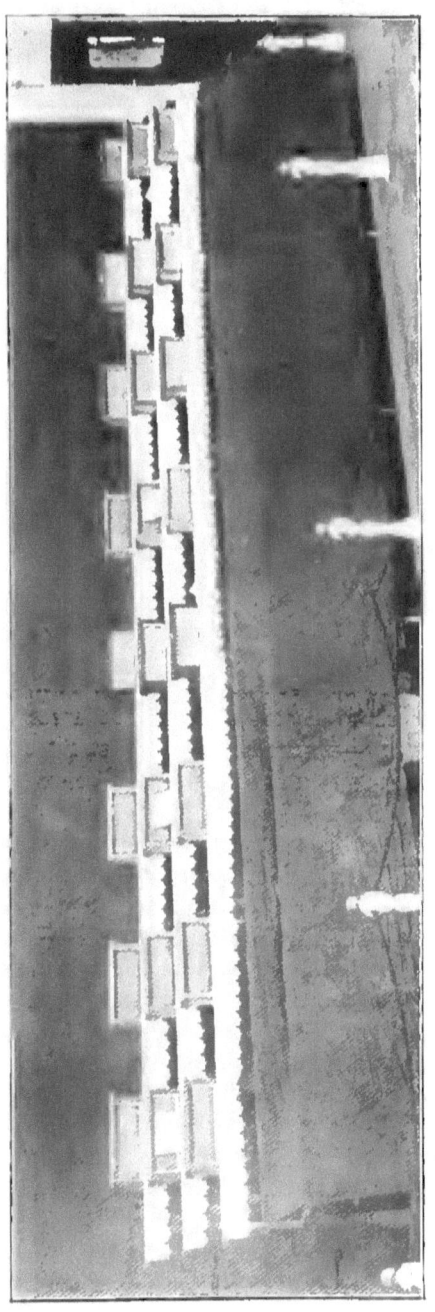

A Record Shallow Comb Class, Grocers' Exhibition at the Agricultural Hall, London, 1911.

Vinegar and Mead.—These need little explanation. They are not extensively shown, and a great deal depends upon the palate of the judge. Vinegar should be well matured and free from the crude taste of acetic acid. It should be sour with no tendency whatever to sweetness, a fault often present. It should be quite clear and free from all traces of vinegar plant or sediment.

Mead also should be well matured, clear, bright, and sparkling. If fortified with spirit it should be disqualified. It has a characteristic flavour and bouquet, and should be neither too sweet nor have any acid flavour about it..

Cakes should be plainly made with a distinct flavour of honey. They should be light and even in colour right through, with a close grain. To judge cakes properly it is necessary to cut them right through the middle, see Fig. 12. This will often expose faults in texture and colour which otherwise would not be seen.

Confectionery, Medicines, etc., should be judged according to their several merits. They are exhibits which do not appear often enough on the show bench.

Fig. 12. Cake cut for judging.

Observatory Hives.—These should be well constructed to avoid sacrifice of bee life. There must be proper spacing between frame ends and side of hive, also between glass and face of comb. The face of every comb should be easily seen. The presence of a fertile queen should be assured, taking account of her age. Worker, drone, and queen cells should be present, the two former filled with eggs and brood in all stages. Proper ventilation should be noted and the judge should satisfy himself as to the absence of disease. To ascertain this with certainty it will be necessary sometimes to have the glass removed and the combs taken out. The hive should not be too crowded, but sufficient bees must be present to maintain the necessary heat for the well-being of the brood.

The occupants should consist of the three kinds of bees. To detect the queen quickly it is well to remove one shutter

A Japanese Honey Jar.

some little time before commencing to judge, as she generally makes for the dark side and can then be found more quickly when that shutter is removed for inspection.

Trophies.—The general taste and get-up of the honey, together with design, should be taken into account. Honey

48 PRODUCING, PREPARING, EXHIBITING

in all forms and of all kinds should be present. The inclusion of products and flowers will depend upon the wording of the schedule and also the form of trophy, whether intended for a shop window display or otherwise. The receptacles should be those generally used in commerce. Above all, cleanliness should be strictly observed.

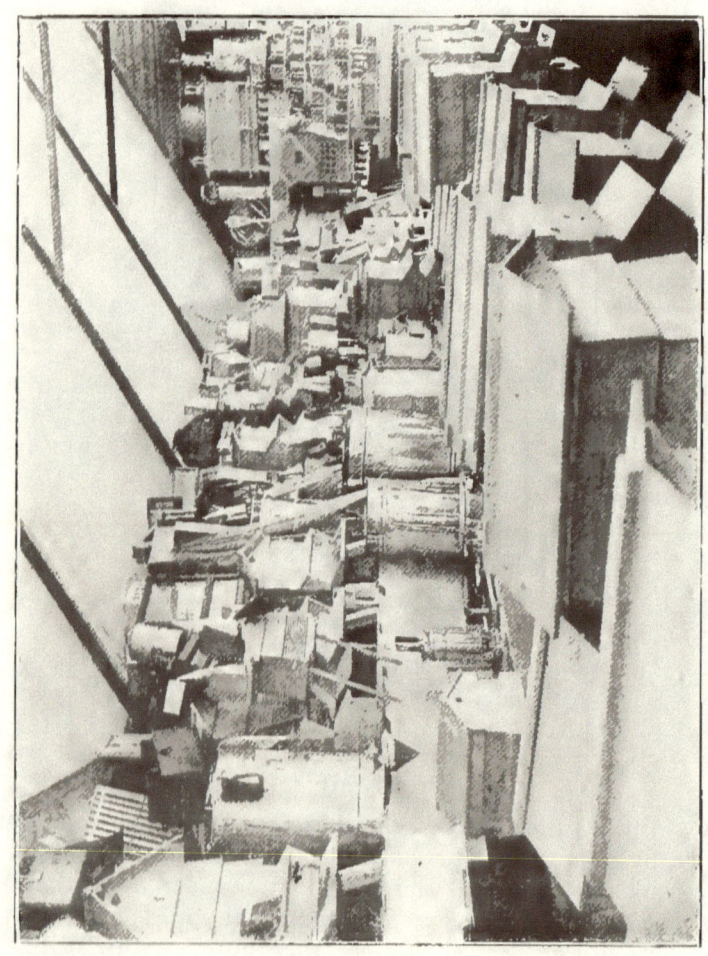

A Corner of the Appliance Classes, Lincolnshire Association Show, Brigg, 1901.

Hives and Appliances.—These should be carefully examined for accuracy and good workmanship, even to the minutest detail. A rule or gauge should be used for testing measurements. The quality of the wood must be noticed, sap, knots, and other faults should be absent, the material being of yellow pine. The simpler the hive or appliance is in working the better. Fads and complications should not count but be discouraged. The prices at which the goods are listed should also be noted, and points deducted either for an outrageously expensive article or one that is put in below the actual cost price merely for the sake of capturing the prize for advertisement purposes. In both cases, if prizes are awarded, a false impression is given to the public as to the actual cost of bee-keeping.

Whenever possible all the prizes offered should be awarded for the purpose of encouragement, but if the exhibits are inferior and not worthy of mention there should be no hesitation in withholding prizes with the object of avoiding giving a wrong impression, as already stated. In exceptionally large or good classes it is sometimes advisable to grant extra or special prizes. Non-competitive exhibits, which usually add to the attractiveness of a show, are also encouraged by due recognition on the part of the judge, for a great deal of expense and trouble are often expended upon them by the exhibitor.

CHAPTER V.
Judging by Points.

Not only in apiculture, but in many other branches of exhibiting, a great deal of nonsense is said and written, more especially by novices or those who know very little about the work. Some advocate a hard and fast point schedule, but this is absolutely impossible for many reasons. Take, for example, aroma. How is it possible to standardize the olfactory senses of each judge or unify the sense of flavour?

It would be quite possible to have a standard for colour, but hardly for density. A judge would frequently be criticised for inconsistency, not only at separate shows, but also in various classes of the same show. For instance, at one show at which he was officiating he might commence judging on a fairly cool morning, part of his work being done before he went to lunch. In the meantime the tent or building has become heated by the sunshine, with the result that when he resumes his duties some of the honey will have become much thinner, and would consequently receive lower marks than the same samples judged in the morning. Of course, the exhibitor never takes such a contingency into account.

By remelting the honey between shows, the flavour, aroma, and even colour may be spoilt, yet the exhibitor declares it is exactly the same honey as shown before, and he consequently grumbles because he is placed lower than an exhibitor whom he had beaten previously on points. Slight granulation may also be seen at one show which was not present at the previous one. In granulated honey I have seen cases where, through exposure and other influences, slight fermentation had taken place on the surface of the honey between the two shows. There may be also cases of grumbling by an exhibitor at his non-success owing to a broken bottle at one show having been replaced by one containing honey of an entirely different character, the exhibitor averring that it should make no difference to the judging. Sections perfectly sound at one show may by constant travelling become damaged and leak badly, thus spoiling their appearance altogether. Granulation may also take place and reduce the number of points awarded.

Mr. R. Allen's Exhibit (not for competition) at Brackley, 1911.

To wax that has been re-moulded after long exposure in showing, an entirely different character is given, both to the aroma and hardness, yet it is repeatedly stated to be "exactly the same wax as shown before," no mention being made to the fact of its recent manipulation.

A wise judge will refuse to be tied down by hard and fast rules, but will make his awards on points of his own

52 BEE PRODUCE.

arranging, by the only safe method of arriving at those points, *i.e.*, by comparing the exhibits placed before him at any one particular time. He should also refuse to fill in cards with the points awarded to each individual exhibit for the reason stated, and also on account of the endless

Noted Prize Winners: Mr. and Mrs. J. Pearman.

time involved in the work of doing this. He will otherwise lay himself open to endless criticism by his varying awards in the various classes and at different shows, which are bound to occur. At some of the large shows it would take the judge a couple of days to do all this, for in many cases from one hundred to two hundred exhibits are staged. A point card is of no use to an exhibitor who cannot attend

The Largest Class of Light Extracted Honey ever shown in this country. Seventy-five exhibits (900 jars) on staging eighty feet long, Grocers' Exhibition at the Agricultural Hall, London, 1911. On the left is seen Mr. E. H. Taylor's Appliance Stand.

and compare his exhibit with the others staged in competition with it. Very few exhibitors attend the shows, so the card teaches them nothing, and only serves to make them discontented with the varying points awarded at different times.

The fallacy of hard and fast point judging has been proved and given up in the case of horses, cattle, and poultry. Those who write favouring this system show an utter ignorance of the practical side of the subject, and try to hide this by a comparison of what they term the " inconsistency of the judge." Those who have attempted this system deserve all the adverse criticisms written about them for their foolishness in endeavouring to attain what is impossible.

That the comparative method of judging is a reliable one has been repeatedly proved. Here is a definite example. In 1910 Mr. Ernest Walker was one of the judges of honey at the Grocers' Exhibition, and also the sole judge at the Dairy Show. Many of the exhibits at the former were shown at the latter, and in every class where this was the case he placed the winning exhibits in the same order of merit. The following year he judged both shows alone, and did exactly the same thing.

CHAPTER VI.

Producing and Preparing Extracted Honey.

In this category I deal first with those methods of preparation which apply equally to all kinds of honey, with the exception of grading for colour and flavour.

First, absolute cleanliness is essential for success. The jars should be carefully chosen of clear white glass, free from all air globules and bits of black ingrained in the glass

Noted Prize Winners: Mr. and Mrs. A. W. Weatherhogg.

or other blemishes often seen in the cheaper kinds. To secure the best, a little extra money will have to be expended in obtaining jars of English made flint glass. These are undoubtedly the best. For preference I would use square jars—they pack more easily, and the corners reflect the light through the honey, making it appear brighter. They should have a screw cap made of good hard metal, which must fit well to prevent leakage, but it should not be screwed down so tightly as to be impossible for the judge to move it with his hands. This is sometimes done and may result in the exhibit being passed over. Instead of a cork wad, frequently badly cut, and having loose particles upon it which are apt to get into the honey, use one made of white pasteboard. Such wads are cleaner, and reflect the light down into the honey. This is a small

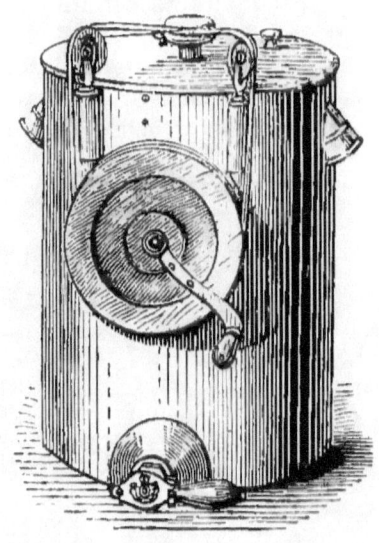

An Old-fashioned Geared Extractor, 1875.

matter, but it is such trifles that often carry the balance to success. The jars should be carefully washed in warm soda water, then well rinsed in clear tepid water, and turned upside down on a rack in front of a fire until they are thoroughly dry, then lay them in the same position in a warm and dry place.

The honey used for showing should be taken from combs that have remained on the hive as long as possible. All the cells should be sealed in order to ensure only ripe honey being obtained. That secured first in the season should be

AND JUDGING BEE PRODUCE. 57

used if possible, for it does not granulate so rapidly as honey gathered later. Care should be taken before uncapping for extracting to wipe all moisture from the knife after its removal from the hot water. This prevents extra moisture getting into the honey and thus reducing its density. After extracting, strain the honey carefully through muslin into a clean ripener. This should then be stood in a copper containing water heated until the finger cannot remain in it with comfort for more than half a minute. Keep the water at this temperature, with the ripener uncovered, for from ten to fifteen minutes. The water must not be allowed to boil or the honey will become discoloured and lose its aroma. Have another ripener ready, which must be clean and well warmed. Strain the hot honey into this, using for the purpose old flannel, which must also be warmed in the oven before use. New flannel should never be used, for bits of fluff will come off and become mixed with the honey. Place the lid on the ripener, and let the honey stand for two or three hours to allow the air globules to rise to the surface. In the meantime well warm the jars either in front of a fire or in an oven. This done, fill the jar and screw down while the honey is still hot, as this will prevent granulation from taking place so soon, and retain the aroma. By adopting this method the work is greatly facilitated, as the warmed honey being thin goes through the straining material much quicker. When running the honey into the jar this should be held at an angle, as in Fig. 13, so that the honey strikes the side of the jar near the top just below the shoulder, and then runs down. In this way air bubbles will be avoided, which would eventually rise and form a scum if the jar were held in an upright position during the operation. Until the time it is intended to send the honey to the show it should be stored in a dark, cool place.

Honey not quite up to the standard can often be improved by legitimate treatment. Superfluous matter can be taken away, but nothing must be added. It is impossible to treat

58   PRODUCING, PREPARING, EXHIBITING

with any advantage samples of a dead colour, or those which contain pollen (such as those taken from skeps) or

Fig. 13. The Method of running the Honey into the Jars.

honey dew. Colour cannot be improved artificially, but flavour may be occasionally by mixing two samples. To do this, great care must be exercised to make them blend properly. Both must be heated separately to be of the same specific gravity before the mixing takes place. If the mixing is done while the honey is cold, and the heating carried out afterwards, the result is not nearly so satisfactory. The greatest improvement is in removing some of the moisture, and making the honey more dense, as this is just the process carried out by bees in ripening honey. This may be done in four different ways : (1) By placing the jar or other receptacle containing the honey in hot water ; (2) By means of a retort in the same way that spirit is distilled; (3) By having a number of large shallow vessels about three quarters of an inch in depth, in which the honey is placed, close up to a glass light, such as the top of a greenhouse, where the sun carries out the work of evaporation. By this method, however, a good deal of the aroma is lost, more especially if the honey remains exposed for a long time; (4) By placing the honey in glass jars, with their caps removed, in a solar wax extractor. Heating the honey not only removes moisture but also brightens it considerably, and if evaporated in the solar extractor (which is the best method) it becomes slightly lighter in colour.

Grading.—This should be carried out in accordance with the requirements of the class in which the honey is to be exhibited. Colour may in the first place be judged to a certain extent by holding the combs up to the light. Their selection should be made in this manner, each grade of colour being kept separate. When extracted, the honey of each colour should be kept separate until the final choice is made. For exhibiting in the light classes it does not follow that the lightest sample must be chosen. A nice, light amber honey is usually the most successful, provided it has all the other points, such as aroma, flavour, and density. Water-white honey, though usually very dense, beyond being sweet is, as a rule, flavourless.

Honey intended for light, medium, or dark classes should be graded by means of the glasses supplied by the British

60   PRODUCING, PREPARING, EXHIBITING

Bee-keepers' Association and *British Bee Journal*, instructions for the use of which have been given on page 19. Medium or dark honey must not contain the least trace of heather honey, unless a blend is distinctly mentioned in

D. M. M. and Mr. Crawshaw Judging at a Northern Show.

the schedule. Nor should granulated honey be shown in any class but that specially provided for it. If granulation has already commenced the honey should be warmed in the jars in the following manner:—Remove the caps and stand the jars in a saucepan or other suitable vessel on slats of wood placed on the bottom, to prevent the jars from coming

AND JUDGING BEE PRODUCE. 61

in direct contact with it. If they did so the honey would be spoiled by being burned, or some of the jars might get broken. Place the jars in position on the slats, pour in cold water until it reaches their shoulders, then put the saucepan on the hob by the side of the fire until the water gets warm, when it can be stood over a slow fire until the temperature mentioned on pages 57 and 61 is reached. A gas ring or a paraffin stove is best for the purpose. Keep the water at the same temperature for from ten to fifteen minutes, remove the vessel from the fire, cover over with muslin to keep out dirt, and, when the jars can be handled with comfort and while still standing in the water, screw down the caps. Allow them to stand until both water and honey become cold, then lift out the jars, dry, and polish them. Even very slight granulation gives a cloudiness which would be fatal to the winning of a prize.

If a thermometer be used, the water should not be heated above 160deg. Fahr. A temperature of 130deg. would do, and is less likely to affect the aroma, but, of course, it would take a longer time to melt the granules. No scum should remain on the honey when in the jars, but in the event of a little making its appearance it must be carefully removed with a hot spoon. This is one of the niceties in the preparation of exhibits showing the skill of the bee-keeper, the neglect of which has lost many prizes. The majority of judges very rightly pass over such carelessly prepared honey without taking further trouble about it. The caps must be scrupulously clean both inside and out, being brightly polished, as should also be the outsides of the jars.

However much care may be expended, there are times when honey in sections and shallow combs will granulate a little. If done carefully it can be liquefied by being stood in a warm place for some time. According to my experience, two of the best places are over the pipes in a hothouse or on the plate rack over a kitchen range. The super containing the honey should be wrapped in newspaper to keep out dust and dirt. The length of time required for liquefying depends upon the extent of the granulation, and the further it has been allowed to go the longer the time that will be required for dissolving all the granules. By either of these methods I have been able to liquefy honey, even when quite solid in the combs. The object is to place the honey for an extended period in a temperature warm enough to liquefy it without melting the wax.

The best honey for light and medium classes is obtained from White Clover, Sainfoin, Mustard, Turnip, and Charlock, while for the dark classes that from Fruit Blossoms, Bean, Blackberry, and Buckwheat is the best. A much lighter and denser honey is obtained from White Clover when grown on a clay soil than from that on a sandy soil, while Sainfoin only thrives where there is a chalk subsoil. Honey for the liquid classes should never be taken from sections, as this is invariably thinner than that obtained from shallow combs.

Granulated Honey.—For this purpose the best honey should be chosen. To obtain the best results it must be thoroughly ripe. For preference it should not be heated at all. Keep the caps on after bottling, and put the honey in a cool place exposed to the light. Turning the jars and occasionally stirring the honey will give it a more even grain, preventing that flakiness which so often occurs at the side of the jar. After granulation has taken place the honey should be stored in a cool, dry place, as warmth is liable to set up slight fermentation. It should be kept at least twelve months before it is exhibited so that it may obtain the solidity which should always be present in a good sample.

Before sending the honey to the show remove the caps, which will have become dull on the outside, and in some cases rusty. With a damp cloth on a knife-blade rub the inside of the neck of the jar carefully just down to the edge of the honey to remove the dark deposit which very often forms there. The screw portion on the outside should

Nottinghamshire Association's First Prize Exhibit, County Honey Trophy Class, Royal Show, Manchester, June 23rd, 1897, with the Secretary, Mr. G. Hayes, and the Author.

also receive careful attention in the same way, for there also a dark deposit is apt to form which, if allowed to remain, quite spoils the appearance of the honey when the cap is removed by the judge. New caps and wads replacing the old ones will complete the preparation and make all look neat and clean.

Sometimes when it is desired to make an exhibit in the granulated classes the bee-keeper finds that he has forgotten to reserve honey in jars for this purpose, but if he has granulated honey in bulk he need not despair but can make his entries. The granulated honey should be warmed slowly

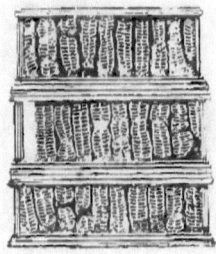

An Old-fashioned Super of Comb Honey, 1876.

in the tin or other receptacle in which it has been placed until it can be moved with a spoon, *i.e.*, to about the consistency of putty. It should then be put into the jars, care being taken to hold the jar at such an angle that the honey may run down the side to avoid air bubbles, which are difficult to remove once they get in. If not quite even in colour warm a little more and stir. The warming is, of course, done by surrounding with water as already described. All being now even in texture, let the honey stand in a very cold, light room, when it will soon harden again.

The best granulated honey is obtained from Clover, Charlock, Mustard, and Turnip flowers.

Heather.—This is one of the finest honeys produced, and that obtained from *Calluna vulgaris*, or Common Ling, is the best. To take out all the bits of wax by means of the press (Fig. 14), it should be pressed through muslin. Heather honey is more liable to ferment than any other kind because, being a late crop, a great deal of it is pressed from unsealed combs. In order to keep it for twelve months, which is necessary for exhibition purposes, as it is obtained too late in the season to be shown much in the year in which it is gathered, it is necessary to be very careful to take it only

Fig. 14. Heather Honey Press.

from combs well sealed. It should be gelatinous in consistency, of a rich amber colour, and free from the rounded granules characteristic of granulated heather honey. It is a difficult honey to liquefy, and if this be attempted it usually results in the honey swelling and running over the top of the jar. To prevent this slight granulation it should be kept in a warm, dry cupboard. The flavour of this honey is a bitter sweet, which should not be too pronounced. Heather honey obtained from *Erica cinerea* is different in density. That from *C vulgaris* can only be taken from the combs by pressing, but that from *E. cinerea*, being thin, can be taken out by means of the extractor. It is obtained in some of the Southern and Midland counties and, as a rule, has a pungent odour, with a mild, pleasant flavour. In competition it does not compare favourably with the former, and rarely obtains premier honours.

Heather Blend.—In the preparation of this honey, as a rule, the bee-keeper is rather puzzled. Judges differ as to whether the heather or clover should predominate, and it would be well if a standard could be fixed on this point. My idea is that to give a pleasant flavour the heather should be in very much smaller proportion, but not too pronounced, for many people object to the strong taste of pure heather honey. Instead of being gelatinous it should have a liquid consistency. An exhibit may be prepared in two ways. That most in vogue is by mixing a small proportion of heather honey with clover honey. In doing this the method already given on pages 57 and 61 of heating both lots must be followed. The other method is by using combs that contained honey from *Erica Cincrea* in the previous year which can be extracted, for the storage of clover honey. This imparts a delicate aroma of heather to the clover honey.

CHAPTER VII.

Producing and Preparing Comb Honey.

Sections are the principal items under this head, although at many shows there are classes for shallow combs suitable for extracting which of course, are judged on the same lines. To obtain good show sections the combs must be drawn, filled, and sealed very quickly, and can therefore only be obtained when the honey flow is at its height. Swarms are best for this purpose; there is also a great difference in the comb-building qualities of different colonies, some doing work of such an unsatisfactory character that the combs are useless for showing, while others are the reverse, and give good, clean, straight combs with even

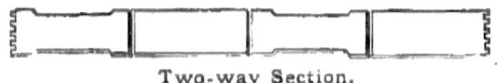

Two-way Section.

capping. To obtain the best results, careful selection and breeding of bees for these qualities must be carried out year after year. While the district may have a great deal of influence on the work, I am certain that the strain of bees has far more, and am convinced that the success of men like Messrs. Woodley, Brown, and Weatherhogg in obtaining such beautiful sections is due mainly to their care and trouble in this matter.

Foreign bees are of no use for the production of first grade sections, as they use too much propolis, and their great tendency to swarm prevents the crowding and husbanding of warmth so necessary when working for comb honey.

The sections used should be those known as "two-beeway," split and grooved. The wood inside should be

68   PRODUCING, PREPARING, EXHIBITING

painted with a thin coat of wax, which will induce the bees to attach the comb all round, and fill the cells to the outer edges. The wax should be put on while very hot by means of a paint-brush, after having made the woodwork warm by placing it in an oven. Care should be taken to avoid the wax getting into the V joints, otherwise the section will not fold square. Sections should be fitted with full sheets of extra thin super foundation, which must only extend to within a quarter of an inch of the bottom, otherwise

Fig. 15. Lee's No. 48 Rack.

buckling may take place. They must be folded square by means of a block, and, before folding, the outside of the V joints must be moistened with hot water, or, owing to the previous drying in the oven, they are liable to break.

The rack used should not be one furnished with T girders, as they prevent the sections from fitting close, allow heat to escape, and propolis to be used in excess. Racks having wooden slats at the bottom about seven-eighths of an inch wide are the best. They should also be built out at the side, so that they may be the same size as the brood chamber and allow of side movement in addition to that at the end. Lee's No. 48 (Fig. 15) is an ideal rack for the purpose.

AND JUDGING BEE PRODUCE.

The followers, with springs at the end and side, keep the sections rigid and square, allowing their removal without damage. The thinnest dividers obtainable should be used, as these allow of close fitting and the conservation of heat. The colony should be overflowing with bees and in such a populous condition that immediately the rack is put on they will take possession of it. A few bait sections used at the side will also induce bees to take to them more quickly. The usual practice of putting these in the centre is not the best, for bees take to the centre sections readily;

A Splendid Class of Sections, the pick of the country, on staging forty-five feet long, Grocers' Exhibition at the Agricultural Hall, London, 1911.

the difficulty is to get them to work in the outside ones. If the baits are placed on the outside the bees will fill all the sections more rapidly. Great care should be taken to wrap up the racks very snug and warm, and no crevice which will cause a draught must be left. Plenty of bottom ventilation should also be given by raising the brood chamber three-quarters of an inch all round (Fig. 16). I have found the following plan to work well:—Allow the selected colony to swarm naturally, then hive the swarm in a shallow frame super with ten drawn-out combs having worker cells, and put on this a couple of section racks prepared in the way described. When bees swarm they come out prepared to build comb, and are anxious to do so,

70   PRODUCING, PREPARING, EXHIBITING

therefore the work is carried out quickly with the best results. There being little room below, and no comb-building to do there, the bees go up, build, and fill the sections at once. In either method an excluder should be used, a wire one for preference, as it obstructs the bees less than any other form.

When the sections are sealed they should be removed, because if left longer they will either get travel-stained or the bees are liable to thicken the cappings and so make them unsightly. Use as little smoke as possible during the process of removal, none at all if the bees are quiet, otherwise they will spoil the combs by puncturing the

Fig. 16. Ventilating a Supered Hive.

AND JUDGING BEE PRODUCE.

cappings. Use a Porter escape to clear all the bees out of the rack.

The sections should be graded after removal, rejecting those having too many pop-holes or others which are capped unevenly. Preference should be given to combs having worker cells, as these present a finer appearance. If, however, this is impossible, each exhibit should consist of one kind of cell only, and not worker and drone mixed. For instance, it will not do to have, say, three out of a dozen sections containing drone cells and the remainder worker cells, or *vice versa*. The whole of the twelve should consist of either all drone or all worker comb. The cappings ought not to look greasy, sunken, or have the appearance of having been damped, but should be thin, transparent, and slightly raised. In grading, reserve more than are required to make up the exhibit in case of accidents.

It is necessary to preserve drawn-out comb in order to obtain good heather sections. Clover sections, the combs of which are fully drawn out, but not sealed, can be extracted and kept for this purpose. As in September the weather at night is usually rather cold, it is not conducive to comb-building, therefore if drawn-out combs are given to the bees good sealed sections are more likely to be obtained. If the bees have to build combs it often results in partly-filled sections, the honey remaining unsealed. It is of no use showing honey not well sealed, as is often done in the heather section class.

The colour of cappings on heather and clover honey is white, while that on sainfoin is of a pale straw colour.

More time and trouble is necessary in the preparation of sections than with extracted honey. On no account should granulated comb honey be staged. To prevent this as far as possible, when the sections are removed from the hive they should be well cleaned by scraping the wood and freeing it from all propolis, not only on the sides, top and bottom, but also round the edges. This should be done

A Queensland Bee-keeper's Trophy at Bowen Park Exhibition, 1907.
From the "Queensland Agricultural Journal."

with a piece of glass or a steel scraper, such as cabinet makers use. Small particles of propolis inside the section should be carefully removed with the point of a sharp knife. This done, the sections should be stored in a dark, dry, dust-proof cupboard, and it is better to wrap them in paper before placing them there. They should not be glazed until just before they go to the show, and if they are sent to several exhibitions it is advisable to re-glaze each time to

Making Show Cases at Messrs. Jas. Lee & Son's Factory.

give them a clean and fresh appearance. The glazing should be surrounded by an edging of white lace paper. Colours should be avoided, as their use spoils the appearance of comb honey. An exception can, however, be made in respect to the band surrounding the section, pale blue looking very well in such a case. To make sections look attractive, the woodwork should be covered with a narrow strip of paper pasted evenly around them, care being taken that the ends meet at the bottom.

Sections can be greatly improved in appearance if the

woodwork is cut down before they are glazed in such a way as to bring the glass to within one-sixteenth of an inch of the cappings. This will hide defects near the edges.

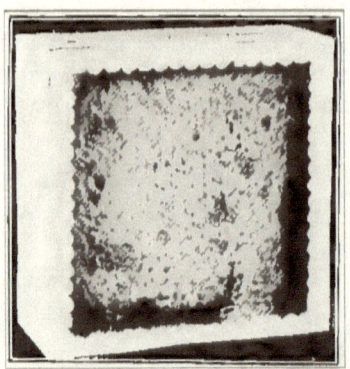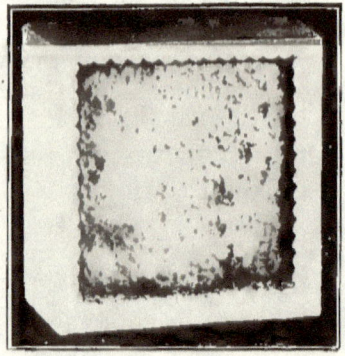

Fig. 17. A Section Glazed Full Width and Cut Down.

Fig. 17 shows this difference, one side of the same section being glazed without cutting down, the other cut down and glazed, as explained. Overlacing should be avoided, as this rule is now strictly enforced at all shows. It is better to err on the right side by leaving a little more than three-and-a-half inches of comb face exposed rather than a smaller surface, and a mistake is often made in trying to lace too closely to the margin. Many prizes have been lost even by old hands owing to carelessness in this respect. (*See* Fig. 18.) Both sides of every section should be tested with the glass template used by the judges. (Fig. 11.) To the majority of bee-keepers glazing sections is difficult work; there is a feeling that a second pair of hands would be useful to hold the glass in position while the lace paper is being put on. The difficulty is overcome by using the neat little machine invented and made by A. H. Wilkes, and shown in Fig. 19. It is so simple that the drawing practically explains itself. It leaves both hands free after the section has been placed in position. As will be seen, the section with the two

Fig. 18. Overlaced and Properly Laced Sections, Grocers' Exhibition at the Agricultural Hall, London, 1911.

76 PRODUCING, PREPARING, EXHIBITING

glasses on either side is first placed in a fairly central position between the rubber-covered discs, the lever is then released, and the section is thus gripped securely; the whole may then be revolved in any direction desired to

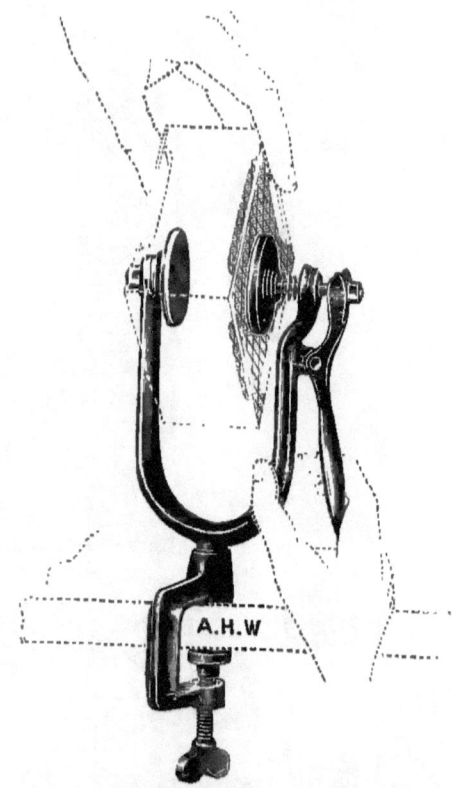

Fig. 19. Wilkes' Section Glazing Machine.

facilitate the fixing of the laced paper. The discs can support a weight of 2lb., and will grip anything from $1\frac{3}{4}$in. to $2\frac{1}{4}$in. thick.

From thirty to forty sections may be glazed per hour, in faultless style, and it is so simple that a child can manage the machine.

Instead of glazing the section itself, cardboard boxes (Fig. 20), into which the sections slip very easily, may be pur-

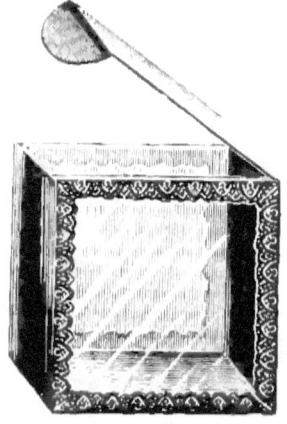

Fig. 20. Lee's Cardboard Show Cases.

chased. If this is done, they should all be of one colour, and not a mixture of glaringly bad ones as in Fig. 50. Each section should be shown in a separate case, and not

Fig. 21. How Not to Exhibit Sections.

in such cases as illustrated in Fig. 21. These are not only unwieldy to stage, but give the sections a very bare, unfinished appearance. The usual $4\frac{1}{4}$ by $4\frac{1}{4}$in. section is the best for showing, as the tall, narrow section which was brought into use a few years ago did not become popular. It was too narrow and top-heavy to stand comfortably on the staging, and as a consequence a great number were broken, owing to their toppling over from the least jarring.

Occasionally, what would otherwise be a good section is spoilt from being of a bad colour. To a certain extent this can be remedied by bleaching, a process first practised by myself, the result of an accidental discovery. Place the sections to be treated in direct sunlight behind one thickness of glass, and where the heat is not too intense, otherwise

Fig. 22. Show Case for Shallow Combs.

they will melt. The lace paper must not be on the section while this is being done, or the pattern will be imprinted in a darker colour round the edges of the comb.

Shallow Combs.—These should be exhibited in suitably constructed show cases, Fig. 22, and the frames should be wide ones with the comb projecting sufficiently beyond the wood to allow the cappings to be easily removed with the uncapping knife. The comb should consist of drone cells, as the larger cells facilitate extraction of the honey; therefore the use of drone base foundation of a substantial thickness and properly wired will give the strength needed to withstand the centrifugal force exerted in the process of extracting. As in the case of sections, the comb should be attached to all four sides of the frame, with as few popholes as possible. The cappings should be thin, perfectly level, and each cell well defined. All the honey should be of an even colour, and not patchy in each separate comb. If more than one comb is shown every one should be alike. Granulation of the honey is a serious fault. To obtain good straight combs, they should be spaced when first put on

A Bell-Glass Super.

one-and-a-half inches from centre to centre until they are drawn out, when the usual wide metal-end can be substituted for the narrow one. If worked by a very strong colony, straight combs will be the result. Another way by which straight combs are assured is by placing thin hanging dividers between the frames.

Bell Glasses.—There are classes for these still at some shows, though the obtaining of honey in bell glasses is a shameful waste of the energy of bees. A flat-topped glass should be used, and for the most attractive appearance the bees should be induced to build the

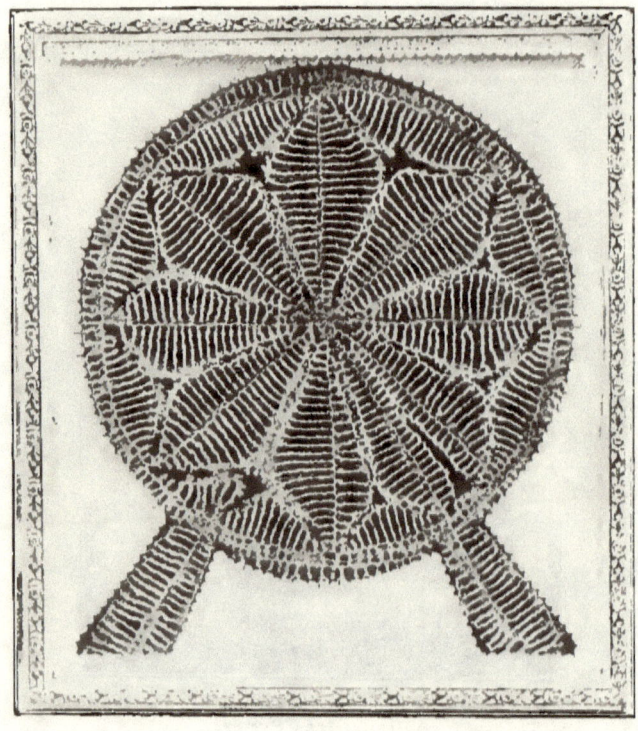

A Honeycomb Design.

combs radiating from the centre, similar to the sections of an orange This can be done by fastening starters at the top in the desired shape. Cut the foundation to fit, then invert the glass in hot water, not allowing any to get inside, and by slight pressure on the warm glass the foundation will stick firmly. It may be found necessary to straighten the combs two or three times during the process of building, and this can be done by raising the bell glass and using a couple of thin, flat pieces of wood.

Honeycomb Designs.—These are, fortunately, not often scheduled, for the same objection applies to them as to bell glasses, although they are effective for advertising purposes. They are obtainable by having a super about three inches

A Honeycomb Design.

deep, with a glass top, upon which foundation is fixed in the desired pattern, by the method shown in the two illustrations.

Classes for Single Jars or Sections.—These prove a great attraction to exhibitors, as they are usually open to all. No fee is charged, the honey being retained by the show authorities, and usually presented to hospitals or other charitable institutions after the show is over. The prize money being large, it is not unusual to have from twenty to forty exhibits in one class. Apart from their attractive-

BEE PRODUCE.

ness, they should be adopted whenever possible for their value for charitable purposes. Not only do they help to alleviate suffering, but they often enable some poor creature to enjoy one of Nature's greatest feasts.

Sale Classes.—These are excellent for the disposal of honey, and it is a pity that such classes are not more frequently adopted at shows. It is true that exhibits of single dozens may be entered for sale, but the above classes are intended for the disposal of honey in bulk, by means of the specimen sample exhibited.

CHAPTER VIII.

Producing and Preparing Wax.

This is one of the most difficult products to prepare in a satisfactory manner. If intended for showing, all new comb and cappings should be carefully saved. The wax must be absolutely clean and of a good pale yellow colour. There must not be the slightest sediment on the bottom of the cake, and when finished it must be free from either honey or water. The former gives a dark speckled appearance at the bottom owing to cavities being formed in the wax. The latter will give a whitish appearance to the

Bee Showing Wax Scales.

wax at the bottom of the mould. To obtain the best results wax should be rendered in a solar extractor, that designed by the late T. J. Weston (Fig. 23) being the most satisfactory for this purpose. In this the wax, after melting, is cleared of the greater part of its impurities in passing through a wire cloth strainer. The action of the sun's rays also improves the colour, while the aroma is retained. Another method of rendering wax is by means of the steam extractor. For other methods of rendering and purifying wax the reader is referred to " Wax Craft," by T. W. Cowan, F.L.S.* After the wax has been rendered and freed

---
* "Wax Craft: all about Beeswax, its History, Production, and Adulteration." (British Bee Journal Office.)

84 PRODUCING, PREPARING, EXHIBITING

from the sediment by scraping it off the bottom of the cake, it is necessary to mould it. For this purpose the plainer the mould the better. Fancy moulded wax, as shown in Fig. 24, entails a great deal of trouble in the preparation, and it can very rarely be made neat enough to

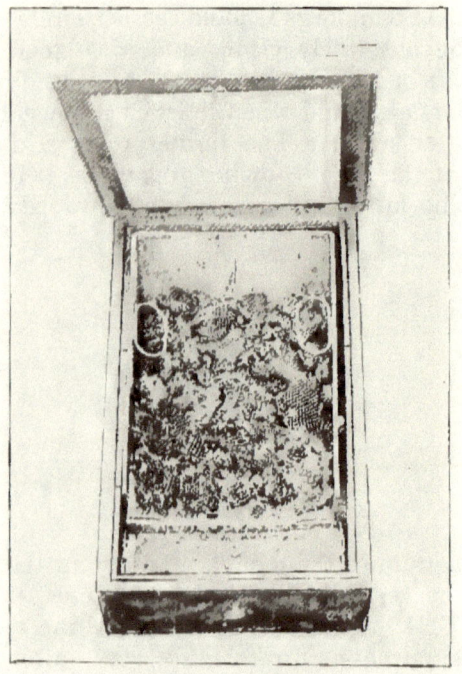

Fig. 23. Weston Solar Wax Extractor in Use.

look well. It is better to cast the wax in one-pound cakes, as this is the usual weight stipulated in the schedules, and it allows of the wax being used at different shows, as the number of cakes required frequently varies. The wax for each cake should be weighed out and melted separately. The best shapes are obtained by using a soup plate or pie

AND JUDGING BEE PRODUCE.   85

Fig. 24. Not the Way to Mould Wax.

dishes of different forms, as seen in Fig. 25. The wax should be melted in a porcelain jar, and for this purpose a two-pound white jam jar answers admirably. This should be stood in a saucepan of soft water and placed over the fire. A couple of pieces of flat iron placed in the saucepan will keep the jar clear of the bottom and prevent breakage by jarring while heating. When the wax has melted, place the mould in a large bowl and surround it with hot water until it just floats, as shown in Fig. 26. To prevent the wax from sticking to the mould, this should be washed out with a solution of soft soap and water. Have ready a piece of old flannel shaped like a jelly-bag for use as a strainer.

86 PRODUCING, PREPARING, EXHIBITING

It should be warmed in the oven to allow the wax to pass through more readily. Fix this bag, or get someone to hold it over the mould, then pour in the wax, and it will pass through as readily as water. This operation is shown in Fig. 27. The wax must be made very hot, but should not boil as this would spoil the colour, texture and aroma. The weight of the wax will hold the mould down. Sufficient hot water should be poured into the bowl to reach to within a quarter of an inch of the top of the mould. Wait

Fig. 25. Wax Properly Moulded and Protected in Glass-topped Boxes.

until a thick crust of congealed wax forms on the top, then pour water heated to the same temperature as that it already contains into the bowl until it flows over the wax. Allow it to stand, and on cooling the cake of wax will float out of the mould, and should then be allowed to remain in the water until cold. The work must be carried out in a very warm room, and, provided that the directions given are carefully followed, a perfect cake of wax free from cracks will be the result. The wax must cool gradually, otherwise it will crack. Plain cakes can, if so desired, be polished by means of a silk handkerchief, but it is not advisable to do so. Nothing but rain or distilled water should be used in the operation, whether it comes into actual contact with the wax or not. In the preparation of wax, the vessel containing it must not come in direct contact with fire heat, such as, for instance, placing the jar on the hot plate of the oven, or it will be spoilt. Whatever method may be adopted, the receptacle for the wax must always be surrounded by water or steam. Avoid making a number of thin cakes, which generally get broken in transit or when in contact with each other, and the edges may become badly chipped, thus spoiling their appearance. In order to retain the aroma, and keep the wax clean, it should be kept

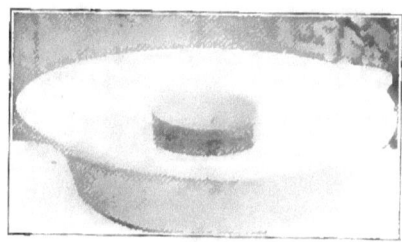

Fig. 26. Mould for Wax standing in Bowl of Water

in an airtight box, both before forwarding to and also at the show. The best method of exhibiting is to put it into neat boxes having a glass lid which can be easily opened. Several good examples are shown in Fig. 25. Such boxes help to keep the wax clean, but the wood or cardboard used for making them should be odourless, otherwise the wax may become affected. Wax that has lost its aroma can be improved by re-melting, and during the process adding a little honey to it, that from heather being selected for preference owing to its stronger odour. The colour of the wax should be a nice clear yellow, lemon or primrose. The cakes should also have a bright appearance, and be free from the slightest sign of dirt. The wax should be brittle, and break with a fine-grained shell-like fracture.

88   PRODUCING, PREPARING, EXHIBITING

Fig. 27. The Method of Straining Wax into a Mould.

It must not be soft and plastic until it has been kneaded for some time between warm fingers.

The classes for " wax prepared for the retail trade " give scope for displaying the ingenuity of the exhibitor.   During recent years the exhibits in these classes have considerably improved. Cases are required, and the cakes placed in them should vary in size, and weigh half an ounce, one ounce, two ounces, and four ounces. The price of each size should also be stated. The cakes should not be square, for if these are packed closely it is difficult to get them out of the case without chipping the edges. For a lady's work-basket square sharp edges are a nuisance, and round cakes are possibly the best for this purpose. A good mould for making these can be made by boring holes of varying sizes in hard wood, such, for instance, as oak, and casting

Fig. 28. Exhibits of Wax for Retail Trade properly Staged.

the cakes in these moulds. Damp the inside of the mould with soft soap solution, or rub with glycerine, which will prevent the wax from sticking and allow the cakes to come out easily. Another good method is to use egg-cups. These are merely suggestions, and no doubt most bee-keepers will have some sort of mould ready to hand which they can use, but it must be borne in mind that the cakes must be compact, and in every case fancy moulds should be avoided. The cakes should be plain, and look like commercial articles. It is useless to send cakes only of one size, or to just put them loosely into a box without any attempt at arrangement. Nor should the choicest sample of wax be used for this purpose, but a good commercial wax, such as would be sold in the usual way of trade, is the most suitable. The casting of the cakes, their arrangement and neatness of the case, are the points which count most. Fig. 28 gives a good idea of how the exhibit should be prepared, and

Fig. 29. Exhibits of Wax for Retail Trade not properly Staged.

Fig. 29, by way of contrast, how it should not be done. In this case, one of the exhibits was of a chocolate colour, and this fault, added to the careless casting and arrangement, made it an absolute waste of money both as regards the entry fee and carriage, for such an exhibit does not stand the slightest chance of winning a prize.

CHAPTER IX.

Producing and Preparing Bye-products, with Recipes.

Vinegar.—This should be brought more prominently before the public, for it is so easy to make, and in its manufacture unsaleable and unripe honey may be utilised. It should be of a light amber colour, free from vinegar plant and sediment, not too acid but pleasantly mild, emitting a pungent odour when the bottle is opened. That which acquires an acidity similar to that of acetic acid should be left at home. It looks best when shown in plain white bottles, holding a pint. One is apt to wonder why an article so easily made is not more in evidence, for, as a rule, the vinegar class at shows is badly supported.

Recipe for Honey Vinegar.—To every gallon of water add two pounds of honey. Pour into a cask or other open vessel and work with yeast or bee-bread taken out of combs. Protect from insects with cream cloth or muslin. If possible introduce vinegar-plant and expose to the heat of the sun. The temperature should be at least 70degs. It should be ready for use in six or eight weeks.

Mead.—Not being a commercial article, this is not frequently exhibited at shows, and many do not even have a class for it. It should be made from the best recipe, *i.e.,* four pounds of best honey to each gallon of water. Washings from cappings, which are frequently used, give only indifferent results. The ingredients in the water should be only honey and lemon, and the necessary quantities of chemical salts. All other substances so often recommended must be avoided. Mead must be at least three years old before it is shown. It should be exhibited in plain white glass bottles, holding a pint, and not in fancy ones or decanters. Do not fortify the mead with spirit, but show it in its pure unadulterated state. It should be of a nice light amber colour, about the

A Monster Display of Honey in a London Shop Window.

same tint as that of whisky, very bright in appearance, and not too sweet in flavour.

Recipe.—To every gallon of water put two, three, or four pounds of honey (according to the quality of mead desired), adding the peel of two lemons to each gallon. Boil for half an hour, and then pour into a cask. When lukewarm add a little yeast, and to a nine-gallon cask two ounces each of phosphate of ammonia and cream of tartar. Tack cream cloth or muslin over the bunghole. When the mead has ceased working bung up the cask tightly, and let it thus remain for six months, after which it can be bottled and must be corked immediately.

Honey Products are those in which honey is an ingredient, and consist of sweets, confectionery, and medicines, the selection being left to the discretion of the exhibitor. In every case the flavour of honey should be distinctly perceptible.

Cakes.—Here again we have articles neglected at most shows, but which if better known would have as a result the employment of a far larger quantity of honey. Cakes should be light and well baked. All flavouring matter, such as almonds, ginger, and carraway seeds should be avoided, for they disguise the flavour of the honey. Plain cakes are the best, and even fruit should be used sparingly. In mixing, the batter should not be too thin, otherwise when baked the honey in them will sink to the bottom owing to its heavy weight, and give that part of the cake a dark appearance, the top remaining of a lighter colour. The cake should be slightly moist, with a fine grain. In showing, it is advisable to put the recipe from which it is made along with it. The following recipes are good, and cakes made from them have won many prizes.

Honey Cake.—Four eggs, five cups of flour, two cups of honey, one teacupful of butter, one cup of sweet milk, two teaspoonfuls of cream of tartar, one teaspoonful of soda, one pound of raisins, one pound currants, half pound of citron, one teaspoonful each of cloves, cinnamon, and nutmeg. Bake in a large loaf in a slow oven. This will be nice several months after baking, or when fresh.

Honey Competitions at the Grocers' Exhibition, St. George's Drill Hall, Newcastle, Nov. 5th, 1902.

Honey Sponge Cake.—One large coffee-cupful of honey, one cup of flour, five eggs. Beat the yolks and honey together; beat the whites to a froth; mix, stirring as little as possible, flavour with lemon juice or lemon extract.

Soft Honey Cake.—One cup of butter, two cups of honey, two eggs, one cup of sour milk, two teaspoonfuls of soda, one teaspoonful of ginger, one teaspoonful of cinnamon, four cups of flour.

Ginger Honey Cake.—One cup of honey, half a cup of butter or dripping, one tablespoonful of boiled cider in half a cup of hot water (or half a cup of sour milk will do instead). Warm the several ingredients together, and add one tablespoonful of ginger and one teaspoonful of soda sifted in with flour enough to make a soft batter.

Honey Fruit Cake.—Half a cup of butter, three-quarters cup of honey, one-third cup of apple jelly or boiled cider, two eggs well beaten, one teaspoonful of soda, one teaspoonful each of cinnamon, cloves, and nutmeg, one teacupful each of raisins and dried currants. Warm the butter, honey, and apple jelly slightly, add the beaten eggs, then the soda dissolved in a little warm water; add spices and flour enough to make a stiff batter, stir in the fruit and bake in a slow oven. Keep in a covered jar several weeks before using.

Honey Cake.—Half a breakfast-cupful of sugar, one breakfast-cupful of sour cream, two breakfast-cupfuls of flour, half teaspoonful of carbonate of soda, half pint of honey; mix the sugar and cream together, dredge in flour with honey, stir it well so that all the ingredients may be thoroughly mixed, add the carbonate of soda and beat the cake well for another five minutes. Put it into a buttered tin and bake from half to three-quarters of an hour.

Confectionery generally consists of sweets and biscuits of various kinds, lemon curd, etc.

Medicines are also staged in the variety classes, and they should contain a large percentage of honey. Below are given numerous recipes for making exhibits of this description. They should always be put up very neatly and in an attractive manner.

Honey Popcorn Balls.—Take one pint of extracted honey, put it into an iron frying pan, and boil until it is very thick; then stir in freshly popped corn, and when cool mould into balls. These will specially delight the children.

A Portion of the Honey Exhibits at the Royal Show, Norwich, 1911.

Honey Ginger Snaps.—One pint of honey, three-quarters pound of butter, two teaspoonfuls of ginger. Mix and boil a few minutes, and when nearly cold put in flour until it is stiff. Roll out thinly and bake quickly.

Honey Shortcake.—Three cups of flour, two teaspoonfuls of baking powder, one teaspoonful of salt, half cup of shortening, one-and-a-half cups of sweet milk. Roll quickly and bake in a hot oven. When done, split the cake and spread the lower half with butter and the upper half with half a pound of the best flavoured honey. (Candied honey is preferred. If too hard to spread well it should be slightly warmed, or creamed with a knife.) Let it stand for a few minutes, when the honey will melt gradually, and the flavour permeate the cake. This should be eaten with milk.

Honey Caramels.—One cup of best flavoured extracted honey, one cup of granulated sugar, three tablespoonfuls of sweet cream or milk. Boil to "soft crack," or until it hardens when dropped into cold water, but it must not be too brittle, and just hard enough to form into a soft ball when kneaded by the fingers, stir in a teaspoonful of extract of vanilla just before taking off the fire and pour into a greased dish. Let it be half or three-quarter inch deep in the dish, and as it cools cut into squares and wrap each square in grease-proof paper, such as grocers use for wrapping butter in. To make chocolate caramels stir in to the foregoing one tablespoonful of melted chocolate just before taking it off the stove. For chocolate caramels it is not so important for the honey to be of the best quality.

Honey Cheese.—One pint of strained honey, the yolks of six eggs, the whites of four eggs, the juice of four lemons, the grated rind of two lemons, three ounces of butter. Stir the mixture over a slow fire until it thickens. It will keep for one year in a cool place, and is very nice for tarts, etc.

Rich Honey Biscuits.—One and three-quarter pounds of flour, three-quarter pound of butter, half pound of light honey, half pound of fine sugar, two eggs, two teaspoonfuls of baking powder, two teaspoonfuls of cornflour, half teaspoonful of salt.

Honey Cookies.—Mix a quart of extracted honey with half a pound of powdered white sugar, half a pound of fresh butter, and the juice of two oranges or lemons. Warm these ingredients slightly, just enough to soften the butter, and then stir the mixture very hard, adding a grated nutmeg. Mix in gradually two pounds or less of sifted flour, make it into a dough just stiff enough to roll out easily, and beat it well all over with a rolling pin; then roll it out into a large sheet half an inch thick, cut it into round cakes with the top of a tumbler dipped frequently in flour, lay them in shallow tin pans slightly buttered, and bake.

Lemon Curd.—Quarter pound of butter, three-quarters pound of fine sugar, quarter pound of light honey, six eggs, the peel of one lemon and the juice of three. To the butter add the sugar and honey, next the peel (grated) and the

Outdoor Lecture by the Author at the Annual Show of the Crayford Bee-Keepers' Association.

juice of the lemons, and lastly the eggs well beaten. Boil till it begins to curd, allow it to cool, then cover. Store in a cool, dry place.

Clarified Honey.—Clarified honey is obtained by taking a jar of granulated honey, place in a pan of hot water (not too hot), and when melted, if necessary, strain through a piece of flannel previously wrung out in boiling water.

Vinegar of Squills.—This can be purchased at any chemists, or you can make thus: Bruised squills two-and-a-half ounces, dilute acetic acid twenty ounces. Mix, allow to remain seven days, then strain through fine muslin. Used for making oxymel of squills.

Oxymel of Squills.—Take half a pint of vinegar of squills, place in a clean enamelled pan and simmer down to half that volume, then whilst hot add clarified honey and mix together (the honey should also be warm). This is the basis of most cough medicines, and is a reliable stimulant and expectorant, and will be found perfectly safe for children or adults.

A Simple and Effective Cough Mixture.—Clarified honey six ounces, glycerine two ounces, juice of two good lemons. Two teaspoonfuls as required.

Honey and Wild Cherry Cough Mixture.—Oxymel of squills four ounces, compound tincture of camphor one ounce, syrup of wild cherry two ounces, decoction of sennege five ounces. Dose, one tablespoonful three or four times daily.

Honey, Horehound, and Licorice Cough Mixture.—Clarified honey four ounces, syrup horehound two ounces, liquid extract of licorice one ounce, oxymel of squills two ounces, compound tincture of camphor four drams, syrup of tolu one ounce. Two teaspoonfuls when cough is troublesome.

Useful Cough Remedy Specially Suitable for Children.—Clarified honey four ounces, oxymel of squills two ounces, ipecacuanha wine two drams, syrup of tolu one ounce, essence of aniseed two drams. Dose, one or two teaspoonfuls as required. Perfectly harmless.

Honey and Black Currant Mixture, for Throat or Chest.—Take one tablespoonful of black currant jam, pour over this quarter pint of boiling water, strain, and add two drams powdered citric acid, three drams tincture of squills, six ounces of clarified honey. This is also a useful drink in fever cases, leaving out the tincture of squills.

A Valuable Tonic in Anæmic Amenorrhœa.—Clarified honey one pound, saccarated carbonate of iron six drams, sulphate of quinine thirty grains. One teaspoonful three times daily after food.

An Exhibit of Honey Products by Mr. A. S. Dell.

Carbolised Wax and Resin Ointment.—Excellent for burns, scalds, boils, ulcers, etc. Beeswax four ounces, resin in coarse powder four ounces, olive oil five ounces, lard three ounces. Melt these ingredients in a jar, and when dissolved add Calvert's No. 2 carbolic acid three drams, and stir till cold.

A Nice Spring Medicine for Children and Adults.—Precipitated sulphur four ounces, cream of tartar two ounces, tincture of orange two drams, clarified honey eight ounces. Dose, one or two teaspoonfuls in the morning, fasting.

A Useful Laxative Medicine Suitable for Children and Adults.—Fine powdered licorice root one ounce, fine powdered senna two ounces, fine powdered sulphur one ounce, clarified honey eight ounces. Dose, one or two teaspoonfuls as required.

Old Chelsea Pensioner Rheumatic Mixture.—Flower of sulphur two ounces, turkey rhubarb powder half ounce, powder gum guaiacum three drams, powder nitre one-and-a-half drams, mustard half ounce, clarified honey one pound. One teaspoonful every alternate evening; it may also be taken in the morning to regulate the bowels.

Improved Rheumatic Remedy.—Flower of sulphur one ounce, powder rhubarb quarter ounce, acetyl-salicylic acid five drams, clarified honey eight ounces. One teaspoonful twice daily.

Honey as an Article of Food for Infants.—Of all the useful purposes to which honey can be put, there is none so valuable as that in which it is used as an article of food for infants, when we take into consideration that by far the greatest percentage are artificially fed, on milk or farinaceous foods, which are sweetened, or perhaps it would be better to say over-sweetened, mostly with beet sugar, with ingredients most detrimental to infant life, such as ultramarine, etc., which are used to make it a good colour, and which it is to be hoped some day the State laws will prohibit. Thanks to the vigilance of our inspectors under the Food and Drugs Acts we can congratulate ourselves on the purity of our foodstuffs in general, but sugar seems to be one of those things which has hitherto escaped the notice of all public authorities, but perhaps its turn will come, but until that

Berkshire, Third Prize Exhibit, County Honey Trophy Class, Royal Show, Manchester, June 23rd, 1897.

time arrives it will be well to leave sugar out of the daily diet of infants, and use only Nature's finest food, *Pure, Sound, Clarified Honey*, which not only serves the purpose

Huntingdonshire, V.H.C. Exhibit, County Honey Trophy Class, Royal Show, Manchester, June 23rd, 1897.

of one of the best sweetening agents, but is far superior to sugar as an article of food, an excellent aid to digestion, hence a preventative of flatulence, one of the greatest of infantile troubles.

Floor Polish.—Clarified beeswax six ounces, rectified turpentine twelve ounces. Melt in water bath, just dissolving the wax, then add the turpentine and stir. May also be used as a polish and preservative for leather, wood, furniture enamel, etc. If intended only for cleaning furniture it is better to use eight ounces of turpentine and add four ounces of linseed oil.

Bee Candy.—This should be shown in a glass-topped box. It should be so soft as to be easily scraped with the thumbnail, and have a fine grain, but not soft enough to run. For preference it should be medicated. Slovenly cakes moulded in paper are unsightly and very rarely win a prize.

Recipe for Candy.—Six pounds of refined cane sugar, one pint of water, half a teaspoonful of cream of tartar, and quarter ounce of salt. Stir until it comes to the boil, then draw the pan back so that it simmers gently for ten minutes. Remove from the fire and stir briskly until it begins to granulate; as it cools pour into a glass-topped box. Should the candy become burnt it would be unfit for bee food.

CHAPTER X.

Observatory Hives, Appliances, Trophies, and Scientific Exhibits.

Observatory Hives.—In the first place the hives should be of good workmanship. They are shown in two classes, as single comb hives and those having three combs. The latter are most frequently scheduled. Whatever hive is used,

Fig. 30. Single Comb Brice Observatory Hive.

ample ventilation should be provided, which must be so arranged that it can be shut off entirely when desired. The interior of the hive should be made to take the standard frames and a super to contain either sections or shallow frames may be placed above. The best material to employ is either mahogany or oak. Double glass should be used

106   PRODUCING, PREPARING, EXHIBITING

for warmth, and wooden shutters covered with baize provided for the outside. The distance between the glass and comb should be just sufficient to allow the bees to pass freely, and not an inch as is often the case, for if there is

Fig. 31. A Three-comb Observatory Hive made by the Author.

too much space intervening brace combs will be built. The hive should be made to revolve on the base, in the centre of which there is a hole for the passage of bees. A loose tunnel providing free flight for the bees should be made in sections to be adaptable for any width of table on which the hive is to stand. The tunnel should be covered with glass so that visitors to the show can see the bees passing in and out. The top comb should be all honey to provide the bees with food. The two lower combs ought to contain brood of all kinds, *i.e.,* queen, drone, and worker, and every phase of bee life should be shown. The combs must be straight, tough, and well built. There should be a good queen not more than two years old. Care should be taken to notice the race of bees named in the schedule, but if not otherwise specified British bees should be shown. Do not paint the queen or clip her wings. A " Brice " feeding stage and a magnifying lens with a ball and socket joint fixed to the hive are useful. An illustration of a single comb hive is given in Fig. 30, and a three comb hive in Fig. 31.

Trophies.—These are often the main feature of an exhibition, and good prize money should be offered for them. The amount of good honey required, the cost of carriage, and the fact that they must be staged only by the exhibitor, prevent a great many from competing in these classes. Yet with all these drawbacks they are usually well filled. A limit is generally placed on the size and height of the trophy, as also in regard to the weight of honey to be shown, and these particulars should be carefully observed. Undoubtedly glass is the best material to use for the superstructure, as wood is much too heavy and too dark. The object to aim at is to keep the whole exhibit as light and delicate in appearance as possible. There is no need to spend much money on the framework, about five or six sheets of good plate glass, each gradually decreasing in size about six inches, are all that is required. The table can be covered with a neat white cloth, or if expense is no consideration, a mirror forms a very effective base. The edges of the glass should be polished and not left rough, a nice rounded edge being the best. Do not use lace paper round the edges as it soon gets dirty and then presents a slovenly appearance. The first sheet of glass can be sup-

108   BEE PRODUCE.

ported on one pound jars, nine inches high, for the restriction as to size of jars does not apply to trophies. Such jars can now be obtained with a screw cap and look very

Fig. 32. A Well-staged Trophy of Honey.

neat. If preferred, sections can be built up two tiers high, or use one pound jars, placing three at the bottom with one standing on them. The following shelves will not need to be so high and can be supported by ordinary one pound

Fig. 33. A Well-staged Trophy of Honey.

110   PRODUCING, PREPARING, EXHIBITING

jars or sections arranged in a different manner for each shelf. The superstructure or framework should be built

Fig 34. A Trophy tastefully staged, including Honey Products and Flowers.

up first, and the filling-in done afterwards. Build the trophy up to the full height allowed and do not let it appear squat, nor should it be overcrowded with honey. As already stated, let it have a light, delicate appearance. Avoid using fancy jars or very tiny ones; none should be smaller than quarter of a pound, and all must have screw caps. Sections should be used sparingly, more especially towards the top, otherwise the trophy will look heavy. A couple of good shallow combs at the base will give a pleasing effect. Most of the honey should be of a nice light amber colour, with all the qualities necessary in the extracted classes. Exhibitors, however, have curious ideas about this, and often state that effect is the only consideration, at the same time thinking it unfair for the judge to taste or test the samples for density. In one case an exhibitor was very irate with me for passing his exhibit because I found a thick layer consisting of bits of cappings and scum on the top of the honey in each jar when it was opened. He said that I ought not to have opened the jars but to have judged by outside appearance only, as he had only extracted the honey and put it in jars an hour or two before the show, and had not had the time to strain it. It was certainly the finest exhibit staged so far as looks went, but this fault was unpardonable, and I could give it no award. Care should be taken to see that sections are not overlaced. A few jars of different kinds of honey, such as medium, dark, granulated and heather may sometimes be used with advantage. Bell glasses and honeycomb designs should be avoided.

Whether flowers should be used in decoration is often a debatable point among exhibitors, and the schedule should make this clear. For a one day's show, flowers and maidenhair fern used judiciously and in an artistic manner give a pleasing effect, but the tendency usually is to overcrowd the exhibit to its detriment. At a show extending over several days flowers should never be used, as they soon fade in the heat and then present a wretched appearance.

Small cakes of wax are always allowed, but bye-products, such as mead, vinegar, cakes and sweets, are only permissible in some instances, and should, in any case, be used sparingly.

Fig. 35. The Way Not to Stage a Trophy. Note the Sections laid flat.

BEE PRODUCE.

Shop-window displays require different treatment. The dimensions are not the same, and they are viewed only from the front. For these only honey and wax should be used, flowers being omitted. It is difficult to make an

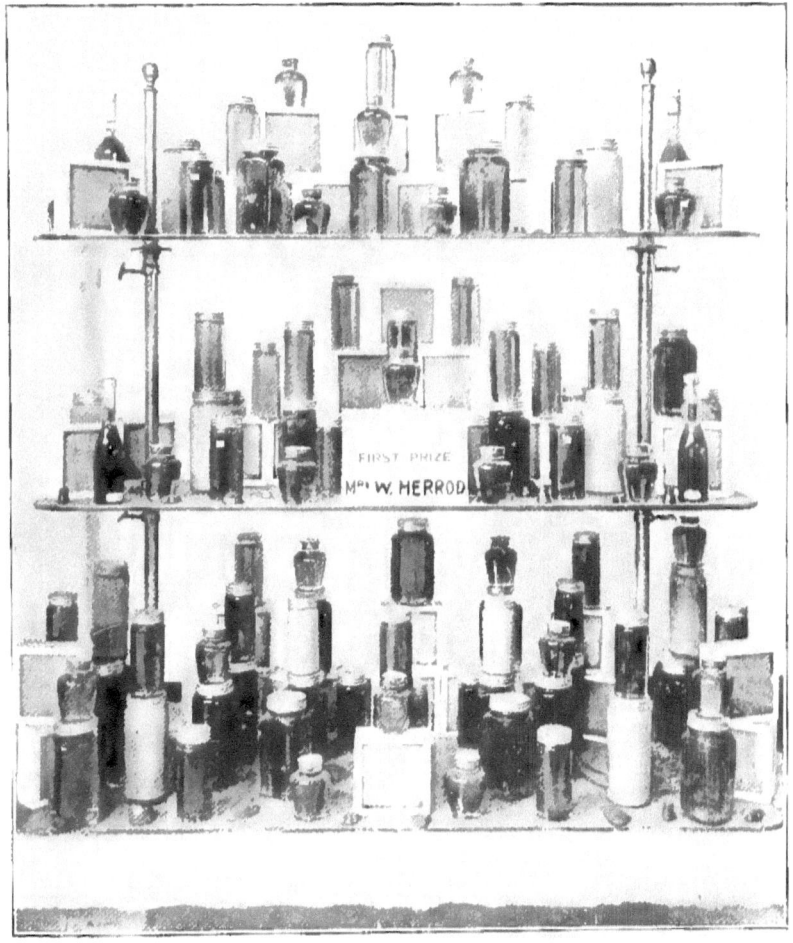

Fig. 36. A Well-staged Shop Window Display, Grocers' Exhibition at the Agricultural Hall, London.

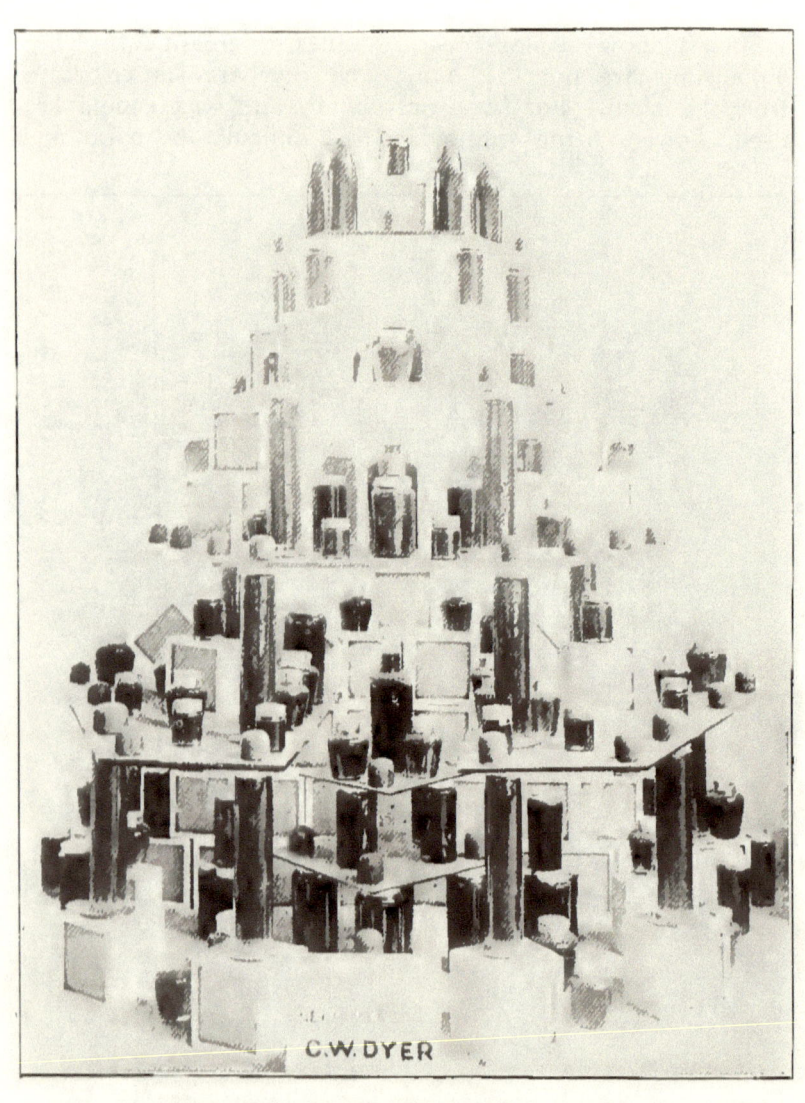

Fig. 37. A Well-staged Shop Window Display, Grocers' Exhibition at the Agricultural Hall, London.

effective arrangement during the rush and bustle in the preparation for a show within a limited time. The writer's practice was to arrange the trophy leisurely at home, then take a photograph of it. With this before him, the exhibitor can put up his trophy in a very short time with the best effect. A good idea of how to build up a trophy may be obtained by studying Figs. 32, 33 and 34, and how not to do it in Fig. 35. Shop-window display, Figs. 36 and 37; how not to do it, Fig. 38. These pictures may make it much clearer than all I have written.

Hives and Appliances.—Classes for manufacturers of bee appliances need little description, although a few words may be useful. Collections of appliances should not be overcrowded, and only goods of a useful and practical nature ought to be shown. A mistaken idea seems to be very prevalent that it is quantity and not quality which tells. While avoiding overcrowding, every article necessary for bee-keepers should be exhibited. The staging of a miscellaneous lot of accessories which are never used or even seen, except upon the show bench, should be avoided, as it gives the novice a false idea as to the number of appliances necessary, and such a heterogeneous collection may prevent him from commencing bee-keeping.

Single hives should be taken from stock, and not got up specially for show. The excessive use of sandpaper and putty, so obvious even to the most inexperienced, should be avoided. Hives must be made of well seasoned wood, free from knots, and all parts be well fitting, even to the minutest detail of frames, division board, metal ends, and the different parts properly nailed. Pay just as much attention to the parts not easily seen as to those exposed. For instance, it is foolish to leave the underside of the floor-board unplaned. Roofs should be made of good stout material, stepped roofs being avoided. Frames should be properly nailed and squared. Avoid fads and complications, and above all do not mark at low prices with the object of obtaining orders. Every manufacturer must

116   BEE PRODUCE.

live, and it is much better to do nothing than to work for nothing and find one's self. It is only the purchaser who benefits by the too keen competition, and even

Fig. 38. A Badly-staged Shop Window Display.

his gain is a doubtful one, for very often he only gets a trumpery article.

Lancashire County Honey Trophy, Indian and Colonial Exhibition, South Kensington, July 30th, 1886.

118   *PRODUCING, PREPARING, EXHIBITING*

Extractors.—These should be well made of block tin. Those geared are the best, and they should run freely and

Fig. 39.   Mr. F. C. Kelley's Home-made Observatory Hive.

quite easily. Lids should be provided, also a well-made easily-working tap, or valve. They should have swinging cages to avoid the necessity of taking out the combs to reverse. This applies to the best kinds, but in the cheaper forms it is impossible to give so much.

Fig. 40. Master Heaselden's Home-made Hive.

Inventions.—These stimulate the inventive faculties of both the manufacturer and bee-keeper, and have resulted

120 PRODUCING, PREPARING, EXHIBITING

in much good in the past, as undoubtedly they will also in the future. They cannot be described but should in every case be simple in construction, useful, and moderate in price.

Scientific Exhibits should consist of things rarely seen,

Fig. 41. Mr. G. W. Judge's Home-made Solar Wax Extractor.

and be described in such a simple manner that even the inexperienced can understand them. If of a microscopic nature, then a microscope should be provided, so that they can be examined.

Educational Exhibits.—A very good educational exhibit is shown in Fig. 39, made by Mr. F. C. Kelley, of Hawarden, to whom I am indebted for the photograph. It is nicely arranged, and, as can be seen, each part of the comb is plainly labelled to show what it is meant to represent. This took first prize at the Cheshire Bee-keepers' Association's Annual Show, held at Chester on August 30th, 1911, and was a source of great attraction to the public.

Included in this class we can have lantern slides, specimens of all kinds of work done by bees, collections of honey from various sources, microscopic slides, specimens illustrating the life history of bees, also their enemies preserved in formaldehyde, and other objects of unusual interest.

Amateur Appliances.—Classes are sometimes provided for these at local shows, and produce good results, being of great benefit as showing how bee-keepers can render their calling more profitable by making their own appliances. As the selection of the appliance is generally left to the exhibitor, fads are occasionally shown. These should be avoided, and only really useful articles exhibited.

Two illustrations of such exhibits are given in Figs. 40 and 41. Fig. 40 is a very well made hive, by Master Heaselden, a boy sixteen years of age, which was shown at the Crayford Bee-Keepers' Association's Show in 1911. Cost in material was eightpence, and it won second prize. Fig. 41 shows a solar wax extractor exhibited in the same class by Mr. G. W. Judge, which was awarded first prize. The cost was as follows: Glass, one shilling and sixpence; tin, eightpence; fittings, fivepence; wood, felt, paint, etc., eightpence; total, three shillings and threepence. In both cases the wood was obtained from old packing-cases.

CHAPTER XI.

Packing Exhibits.

The packing of exhibits is carried out much better to-day than it was a few years ago. The lead taken by the authorities of the Grocers' Exhibition in insisting upon

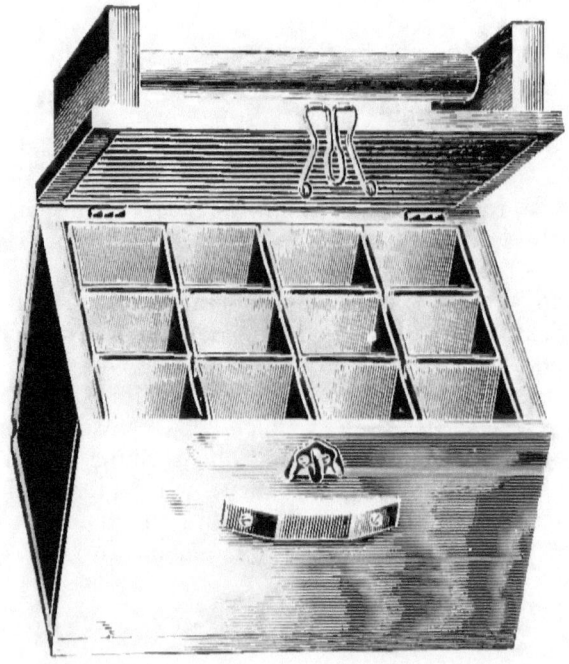

Fig. 42. Travelling Box for Jars.

exhibits being packed in a proper manner has been of great service. Other shows have benefited by it, because exhibitors, having been compelled to furnish proper packing-cases for the Grocers' Exhibition, have used them at others.

It is very little trouble to make a box for extracted honey, as shown in Fig. 42. From such a box it is quite easy for those staging the honey to lift out the jars and place them in position. For safety it is advisable to have a separate cardboard case for each jar, as seen in Fig. 43, because if one jar gets broken the honey is confined to this case and does not run out on to the others, which may happen if they are just put between partitions. Such breakages cause a great deal of trouble, because the only way to get the exhibit clean is to wash all the jars in water. The handle on the box enables it to be moved about easily, and also shows the right side up. There is then no need to label

Fig. 43. Cardboard Cases for Jars in Boxes.

it "this side up." I well remember an exhibit arriving at the Royal Show in a plain box carefully labelled "this side up" on all the four sides. If a proper box is not used, care should be taken to pack in such a way that the jars can be removed without disturbing the packing; this also enables them to be put back again expeditiously. Fig. 44 shows the careless manner in which some exhibitors pack their honey. In this case a shallow box was used, the jars were swathed in sheet after sheet of newspaper, as shown by the one standing alone. The jars being laid down flat, the condition of that exhibit can be better imagined than described. One has unlimited time to wrap up jars in paper at home, but at shows time is valuable, and

124   PRODUCING, PREPARING, EXHIBITING

it cannot be expended upon undoing or wrapping them up in countless sheets of paper. The lids of all boxes should

Fig. 44. Badly Packed Jars, laid on their sides with very little protection either top or bottom of the box.

AND JUDGING BEE PRODUCE.   125

be hinged and fastened with a universal catch, and one good screw is sufficient. The box mentioned above was nailed with three-inch wire nails, and it required a hammer and iron chisel to get it undone, this being only accomplished by splitting up one side of the box. Screws in excess should not be used. Fig. 45 shows a box with only (?) fifteen 2½in.

Fig. 45. Box showing thoughtlessness of an exhibitor using fifteen screws instead of hinges and one screw.

screws in it, instead of having hinges and only one screw. It is also a mistake to put locks on the boxes, as invariably the keys get lost.

Sections should be packed in a spring crate with open sides so that the fragile nature of the contents can readily be seen. (Fig. 46.) This ensures gentle handling on the part of railway porters. At shows where the sections are

126 PRODUCING, PREPARING, EXHIBITING

entered for sale it is inadvisable to pack them in a valuable crate of this description as possibly it may not be returned by the purchaser. A fairly stout box measuring inside about twenty by fifteen inches and a foot deep should be obtained. The sections should be wrapped in newspaper, in two half-dozens, and tied tightly end-ways. The packing material should be good, clean straw, as this gives a more elastic bedding than any other material. Hay should never be

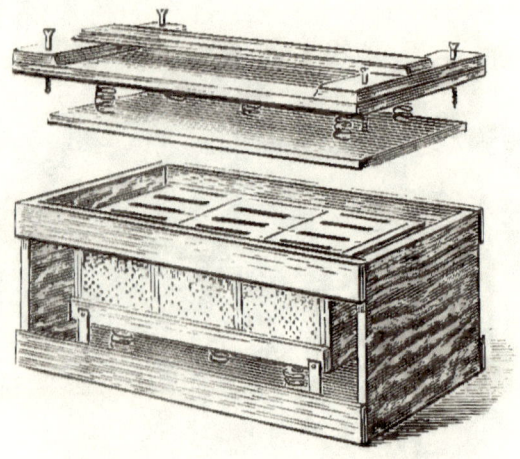

Fig. 46. Travelling Crate for Sections.

used as it is too close in texture, and, as a rule, very full of seeds. A good layer of straw should be placed at the bottom of the box, as this is where the force of concussion comes. The sections should then be placed in position as seen in Fig. 47; this done, they can be packed tightly with straw on two sides and one end. At the other end a cushion made by wrapping soft straw in newspapers and tied with string should be wedged in tightly. Straw is then heaped on the top and the lid forced down and screwed so that the sections are as shown in Fig. 48. When packed in this manner, upon their arrival at the show all that is necessary is to remove the top straw and take out the cushion, the sections can then be lifted out and leave the cavity intact for their replacement after exhibiting.

Fig. 47. Sections Packed in Non-returnable Box, top view.

The important points to observe are, to be sure that there is more packing underneath than on the top of the sections, and that the straw is rammed in tightly all round so that there is no possible chance of them moving.

128   PRODUCING, PREPARING, EXHIBITING

Compare this method with that shown in Figs. 49 and 50, where the sections were sent without any packing either on the top or bottom. The natural result of such a foolish

Fig. 48. Sections Packed in Non-returnable box—side view.

proceeding is shown (as in Fig. 49) by the fate of the sections at the side of the box, all, with the exception of one, being broken.

Fig. 49. The Result of Bad Packing—all the Sections but one smashed.

Fig. 50. Showing Badly-packed Sections in Box, without any material to break concussion; also cases of various glaring colours.

Fig. 51. A Badly-constructed Travelling Crate, showing damage caused by toppling over.

The crate in which sections travel should have a good wide base to stand upon. Some spring crates are made very narrow, the case containing the sections being simply stood on a spring board, and the whole strapped together. These are very unstable, being top-heavy, and they are continually toppling over with dire results, as shown in Fig. 51. A travelling crate for sections having a false top and bottom, with springs, is now made and sold by Messrs. Lee and Son, and is shown in Fig. 52.

Fig. 52. Box Travelling Crate for Sections.

Wax should be packed very carefully to avoid its becoming chipped. The cakes should first be wrapped in paper, then placed in the show cases so that they fit tightly. These in turn should be wrapped in paper and packed with straw in a box. The exhibits for the retail trade class are usually contained in a case. To prevent them from moving, a cushion of some soft material should be made to fit tightly between the glass and cakes of wax.

Hives should be packed in a good stout case with the lid screwed (not nailed), and fitted in such a way that while they may slide in and out readily, they are firm when in position. The supers and other internal parts should be immovably fixed so that they do not rattle about.

AND JUDGING BEE PRODUCE. 131

Each exhibit should be sent in a separate box. This is insisted upon at most shows and helps in avoiding mistakes, as also in lightening the labours of the secretary and stewards. It is very annoying to receive several exhibits packed in one case as shown in Fig. 53. To remove them for staging is quite easy, but when packing up again several exhibits may be put in and the case fastened, when, to the annoyance of the packer, it is discovered that there are yet

Fig. 53. **Wrong Method of Packing : a Number of Exhibits in one package.**

more articles to go in, so the work has to be done all over again. In addition, there is the fact that as such a case is necessarily very heavy, it receives rough treatment on the railway which often results in great damage to the honey. In any case it is fatal to pack jars and sections in the same box.

K 2

BEE PRODUCE.

Exhibits sent by post should not come with a request to have them returned in the same manner, for this may often entail a walk of over a mile to the nearest post office.

As the exhibits in the single jar and section classes are to be retained, these can be sent by post, but they need careful packing. For my part I should not attempt to send sections by post as I find from my own experience that 99 per cent. of them get broken when sent in this way. This does not apply to single jars, as by taking care in the packing they will bear the journey quite safely. Fig. 54 shows how the packing can be done by placing a sheet of corrugated paper round the jar, and narrow strips of wood bound

Fig. 54. A Jar of Honey Packed for Post.

securely in position. It should then be wrapped in another layer of corrugated paper, covered neatly in brown paper, and tied carefully, after which it will be ready for posting. The photograph (Fig. 54) shows a jar of honey sent me from South Africa by post, and which arrived in excellent condition. To avoid breakage by the postal authorities

Fig. 55. Part of the Exhibits Packed for Return, Grocers' Exhibition at the Agricultural Hall, London, 1910.

when obliterating the stamps they should never be put on the parcel but on a tie-on label. Sections by post will need wrapping in many thicknesses of corrugated paper, and even then it is seldom that they arrive intact. In all cases the name and address of the exhibitor should be put inside the parcel in the event of the one outside getting torn off.

I plead specially for care in packing, as the experience of twenty-five years enables me to understand the labour and trouble to which officials are put, irrespective of the loss which continually occurs to exhibitors, by carelessness in this matter. Fig. 55 illustrates the enormous amount of work there is in connection with large shows. These are only a portion of the exhibits packed ready for return from one of the large London shows, where over two tons of honey were staged.

CHAPTER XII.
Despatching Exhibits.

Railway Carriage.—Complaint is very often made about the excessive charge upon returned exhibits. It is obviously impossible for the secretary to undertake to pay the return carriage, even if the money were sent, in order to obtain the cheap rate. The matter rests entirely with the exhibitor. When sending off the exhibit he should obtain from the railway parcels officials a risk note for the return of these goods, fill it in, and hand it to them duly signed. The exhibits will then be returned at the same cheap rate at which they were forwarded in the first instance. As an exhibitor, I only once paid an excessive rate for return. I then learnt my lesson, and since that time have always filled in such a sheet, with the result that the same rates were charged for the return journey. I have been contradicted many times for this statement; therefore, in order that the person despatching an exhibit may know exactly what kind of a note he requires, a copy of that issued by the Great Northern Railway is printed at the end of this chapter. Similar ones are issued by other companies.

There is usually a small charge made for the collection of parcels if the show ground is a long way from the station.

Many exhibitors request that their exhibits be returned by goods train, from the false idea that they get them back cheaper. Anything up to twenty-eight pounds in weight travels as cheaply, and often cheaper, by passenger than by goods train, and there is the advantage of the extra speed of transit. It is, moreover, difficult to get railway companies to collect little odd parcels for goods traffic at a show where they have tons of such goods in large consignments from firms exhibiting to deal with. As a rule, they are in a hurry to get to another show, so the small parcel is overlooked. With regard to passenger traffic the case is dif-

136   PRODUCING, PREPARING, EXHIBITING

ferent, because, as there are a large number of small parcels, a special van is usually sent to collect the lot in one journey.

Addressing.—Address labels and numbers are sent by the secretary, for forwarding exhibits to the show. Good examples are shown in Fig. 56. On the reverse side provision is made for address for the return to be written. This should always be done by exhibitors before tacking the label in position, although constantly they are too careless or too lazy to do so. If omitted, it adds to the work of

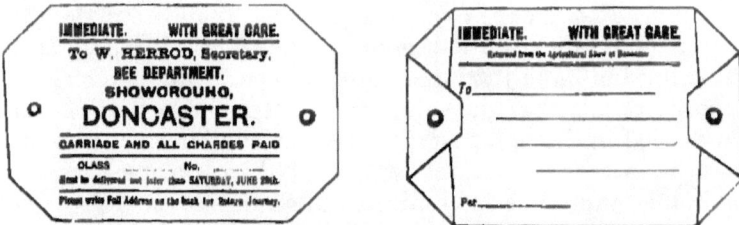

Fig. 56. Front and Reverse Sides of Address Label.

the officials, as they have to hunt for the name in the catalogue before it can be written, at a time when every minute is precious. The address labels and numbers are usually sent in good time, and the secretary should not be worried about a fortnight before the show for them, nor should the exhibit be sent about a week before the show, addressed with a private label and no numbers. It is also inconsiderate for the sender to write and tell the secretary that he has done so, and calmly ask him to " see to it." Numbers cannot be sent until all the entries are in, and the secretary can usually be relied upon to do his work properly. If an exhibit is sent too early it gets knocked about while waiting and trans-shipping from one place to another. The entries should be made in good time, and all will be well. If made by telegram, as is sometimes the case, it is the exhibitor's fault if delay is caused or mistakes are made.

Postcards.—As a rule exhibitors are anxious to learn the result of their endeavours as early as possible. A stamped addressed postcard enclosed with the exhibit will ensure this, as secretaries are usually anxious to give all the assistance they can. The card should be arranged so that as little labour as possible is entailed in filling it in. The class number, also the number of each exhibit, should be written in column form, so that the secretary has merely to fill in the award, as shown below.

This probably seems a small matter, but if one has thirty to forty postcards to fill in without the slightest clue as to what exhibits they refer to, it means that a great deal of time must be spent in hunting out the various exhibitors.

Class.	Number.	Award.
511	20	
512	32	
516	41	

Back of Post Card Ruled and Filled for Results.

It is useless to put in written detailed instructions to those responsible for the staging. As already frequently stated, the time at a show is valuable, and the exhibits should be sent fully prepared. Yet some exhibitors must be ignorant of the work, and act as though they imagine that their's was the only exhibit to be staged.

The following are some of the instructions I have had sent with exhibits: " Please polish my jars and caps before staging," duster enclosed. " Please stage my sections with the best side to the front." " Am not quite sure of the colour of my honey, stage it in the right class for me." " Will you polish my wax before staging? " " My honey has granulated, will you stage it in that class instead of the liquid, in which I have entered?" " Am unable to send sections so have sent an exhibit of wax in its place; please put it right for me." " I have only just bottled my honey, will you please take off the scum? " etc., etc.

The Great Northern Railway Company.

GENERAL AGREEMENT for Perishable and other Merchandise to be carried by Passenger train or by other similar service at Reduced Rates at Owners' Risk.

The Great Northern Railway Company hereby give notice that they have two rates for the carriage of certain Merchandise by Passenger train or other similar service, at either of which rates the same may be consigned at the Sender's option.

One, the ordinary rate, when the Company accept the ordinary liability of a Railway Company; the other, a Reduced Rate, adopted when the Sender agrees to relieve the Company and all other Companies or persons over whose lines the Merchandise may pass, or in whose possession the same may be during any portion of the transit, from all liability for loss, damage, mis-delivery, delay, or detention, except (1) upon proof that such loss, damage, mis-delivery, delay, or detention, arose from wilful misconduct on the part of the Company's servants; (2) in the case of such non-delivery, pilferage, or delay as is hereunder mentioned. The contents of the packages* must be fully and correctly described on the outside thereof in all cases if the reduced rate is to be charged.

If it is desired to have the advantage of the Reduced Rate, it will be necessary to fill up and sign the form printed below, and then return it to the Company.

———————————————————191———

To the GREAT NORTHERN RAILWAY COMPANY.

In reference to the above, $\frac{I}{we}$ request that all Merchandise for which there are alternative rates by Passenger train or other similar service, delivered by $\frac{me}{us}$ or on $\frac{my}{our}$ account at any of your stations, for carriage by railway, may be carried at the Reduced Rates (where and so long as such rates exist) except when specially consigned at the higher rate by consignment note bearing on the face thereof the endorsement "Not Subject to Owner's Risk Agreement," and in consideration of your charging $\frac{me}{us}$ such reduced rates, $\frac{I}{we}$ agree to relieve you and all other

Companies or persons over whose lines the Merchandise may pass, or in whose possession the same may be during any portion of the transit, from all liability for loss, damage, mis-delivery, delay or detention, except upon proof that such loss, damage, mis-delivery, delay or detention, arose from wilful misconduct on the part of the Company's servants.

But nothing in this agreement shall exempt the Company in the case of Perishable Merchandise, as defined by the Railway Rates and Charges Orders Confirmation Acts, 1891-92 (other than Milk, in cans), from any liability they might otherwise incur in the following cases of non-delivery, pilferage, or delay (that is to say) :—

(1) Non-delivery of any package or consignment fully and properly addressed unless such non-delivery is due to accidents to trains or fire.

(2) Pilferage from packages of goods protected otherwise than by paper or other packing readily removable by hand provided the pilferage is pointed out to a servant of the Company on or before delivery.

(3) Delay in transit exceeding forty-eight hours of any package or consignment fully and properly addressed as a result of which the value of the goods is deteriorated to the extent of three fourths if such deterioration is pointed out to a servant of the Company on or before delivery. Provided that in such cases the Company's liability shall not exceed one-half the diminution in the value of the goods.

Provided that the Company shall not be liable in the said cases of non-delivery, pilferage, or delay on proof that the same has not been caused by negligence or misconduct on the part of the Company or their servants.

And $\frac{I}{we}$ further agree to fully, correctly and legibly mark on the outside of every package,* the nature of its contents, and $\frac{I}{we}$ also agree that all packages not so marked shall notwithstanding the foregoing provisions be carried at the Company's ordinary rate.

And $\frac{I}{we}$ further agree that this Agreement shall apply to traffic consigned to $\frac{me}{us}$ from stations on other Companies' lines when the rate charged for the carriage of such traffic is a Reduced Alternative Rate. $\frac{I}{we}$ also agree to the conditions on the back hereof.

This Agreement shall continue in force from the present date until $\frac{I}{we}$ signify in writing to the contrary. Provided nothing herein contained shall prevent $\frac{me}{us}$ during its continuance from sending or receiving any particular consignment at the higher rate should $\frac{I}{we}$ at any time so direct in writing.

Signature of——————————————

Witness——————————————

  this————*day of*——————————191——

* Not applicable to fish, fruit, flowers and vegetables.

N.B.—When a sixpenny stamp is affixed to this Document by the person or firm giving the undertaking before signature, it must be cancelled by such person or firm writing his or their name or title in full across it, together with the date of signature.

CHAPTER XIII.

Showing as a Means of Disposing of Honey.

This can be accomplished in several ways, (*a*) by means of the ordinary classes where a price can be fixed for the sale of the exhibit, (*b*) by means of special selling classes for the disposal of both extracted and comb honey in bulk from samples exhibited, (*c*) by means of trophies in competition, from which the honey is allowed to be sold afterwards, (*d*) a special sale counter in charge of the Association for the disposal of its members' honey. In all cases when the sale is undertaken by the Association a small commission is charged, to cover expenses. (*e*) By hiring space and selling one's own produce from a nicely-arranged stall, as seen in Fig. 56a.

There is no doubt that good returns are made in this way. Although money has to be spent for hiring the space, and time devoted to the selling, there is ample compensation in the extra amount made by saving the middleman's profit. Customers are also secured who write for the honey after the show is over. A good, tasteful display of honey in all forms should be made, and if cups or medals have been won these should be placed in conspicuous positions. Each jar or section sold should be wrapped in a paper with the following printing on it, with the name and address of the bee-keeper at the foot, and with a list of prices at which he sells honey on the back :—

"A WORD ABOUT HONEY.

"*Honey as a Food* is most valuable, proving very strengthening and sustaining to all who use it.

" The weakest digestive organs can take it and obtain nourishment and strength.

" The strong can take it and preserve their health. Before the introduction of sugar, honey was almost entirely used

Fig. 56a. Honey Sale Stall, Grocers' Exhibition at the Agricultural Hall, London, 1910.

as a sweetening agent for all purposes for which sugar is now used; thus it is very useful in the kitchen. Cakes made with honey keep longer than when made with sugar, puddings and porridge become more digestible and nourishing when sweetened with good honey.

" *Honey as a Medicine* is much recommended for coughs, colds, asthma, and all throat and chest affections.

" For weak digestions and constipation in children it is especially useful. Many lives might be saved and constitutions built up by the judicious use of honey in such cases.

" The medical profession are proving the healing and strengthening qualities of pure English honey, and prescribe it more each season.

" Our honey is produced by our own bees in one of the best districts in England, extracted and packed with the greatest care, and is guaranteed absolutely pure."

This will give the purchaser an idea of the value of honey and lead to an increase of sales.

Exhibitors make a great mistake in fixing a ridiculously high price on their exhibits. Should a prize be won, very often a good price may be obtained, simply because it is decorated with a prize card, but for exhibits that have not won a prize such a price as fifteen to eighteen shillings per dozen for sections or jars is exorbitant and prohibitive, and the result is that the exhibit has to go back to its owner instead of finding a customer. About ten shillings per dozen is a reasonable price, and if this is fixed very often sales can be effected.

It is well to bear in mind that the return of an exhibit entails expense, say one shilling and sixpence per dozen, so that even if the honey is sold for ten shillings after its return the actual price ultimately realised is only eight shillings and sixpence.

CHAPTER XIV.

Rules, Regulations, and Schedules.

A difficulty very often arises in drafting schedules and rules for shows. The following will form a guide for Secretaries and Committees, those parts not required being eliminated.

RULES AND REGULATIONS.

For a Large Show.

1.—Exhibits for each Class must be packed and despatched in separate boxes and delivered in the Showyard, carriage paid, not later than Saturday, June 29th, to admit of the staging being completed on Monday, July 1st. The boxes must be so constructed that Jars or Sections can be lifted out and replaced without disturbing the packing, lids hinged and fastened with screws or catch. No nails must be used. Sections or Jars must not be wrapped in separate pieces of paper. A good idea to make the boxes required can be obtained from illustrations on pages 89 and 91 New Edition, British Bee-keepers' Guide Book. Address Labels for the despatch of the Exhibits to and from the Show will be sent to each Exhibitor.

2.—The number of the Exhibit which will be sent by the Secretary (as entered on the Address Label) must be placed on every Exhibit and on each detachable part of an Exhibit, viz:— on the several parts of each Hive, on every section of Comb Honey, and on every Jar of Extracted Honey. The number must be stuck on the jar and not on the cap. No goods will be allowed to be staged unless this Rule is complied with. This regulation does not apply to Classes 510 and 523.

BEE PRODUCE.

3.—No Card (other than those supplied by the Society), Label, Trade Mark, or name of the Exhibitor may be placed upon any part of an Exhibit. Every article exhibited must be bonâ fide the property of the Exhibitor, and all honey must have been gathered from flowers, in the natural way, within the United Kingdom, by Bees the property of the Exhibitor at the time of gathering.

4.—Hives should be securely packed in crates, opening at the top. The top of the crate should be screwed down (not nailed), with as few screws as are necessary for its safe transmission to and from the Show. The various parts of the hive, stand, or floor-board, body-box, super, and cover, should be securely fastened, and a strong cord tied firmly round the hive previous to its being placed in the crate. The legs (if any) of Hives not forwarded in crates should be braced together, and the various parts of the Hives secured and tied as above.

5.—Comb Honey must be glazed on both sides, to protect the honey from the attacks of Bees, or other injury. The glass may be secured by metal clips or with paper edging, which must be of such a width as to leave $3\frac{1}{2}$ inches by $3\frac{1}{2}$ inches of glass clear of paper edging, or in any other neat way capable of easy removal by the Judges. Each Section may be exhibited in a small box with glass on both sides, instead of glazing the Section itself.

6.—All Run or Extracted Honey must be graded for colour according to the standard colour glasses approved and issued by the British Bee-keepers' Association, and be exhibited in plain white glass jars, which must be all of one size in each Exhibit. Granulated Honey must be exhibited only in the Classes for Granulated Honey. Jars must all be effectively secured against leakage to the satisfaction of the Judges, who will be empowered to submit them to any necessary test at the owner's risk. Jars containing Run or Extracted Honey must not exceed six inches in height.

7.—The Council reserve to themselves the right to purchase First Prize samples of Honey at 10s. per dozen, or First Prize Wax at 2s. per lb., or to submit for analysis any Exhibit and to dispose of Honey which may have become damaged in transit, or reduced in value by any other means, at any reasonable price which they may be able to obtain for it, or to return the same to the Exhibitor. If any article sent for exhibition is found to be adulterated the whole Exhibit so sent and the Fees paid will be forfeited.

8.—The selling prices of all articles entered for competition in Classes 511 to 513 inclusive, must be stated in the Form of Entry, which must be properly filled up and signed, and with such form of entry a detailed list of articles comprised in the Exhibit must be furnished. Exhibitors in these classes must undertake to supply at such prices any number of similar articles so included during the ensuing twelve months, at the prices named in their Form of Entry; otherwise the Entries cannot be received.

9.—For Members of the British Bee-keepers' Association, and of the Associations affiliated thereto, the Entry-fee is:—Class 510, 10s.; other Classes, 2s. 6d. each Entry. Non-members of the above Associations will be charged double these fees. No Exhibitor will be allowed to take more than one Prize in any one Class. Any Exhibitor being awarded more than one prize will take his highest award and the lower prizes moved up one to fill the vacancy.

10.—In the event of Exhibitors of Honey of the current year not being able to send their Exhibits owing to unfavourable weather for Honey Gathering, the Entrance Fees will be returned, providing that six clear days' notice has been given of their inability to send these Exhibits. In the absence of Exhibitors, the British Bee-keepers' Association will undertake the Sale of Exhibits. Ten per cent. will be deducted from the amounts received for Sales. Exhibitors in Classes 510 and 523 will be allowed to take orders or sell; in no other class will this be allowed. No Exhibit must be removed until the close of the Show.

11.—Any protest against the decision of the Judges in the Bee Department must be in writing, and be made within twenty-four hours of the time when the Awards are made public. It must be accompanied by a deposit of One Pound. Should the protest be sustained, the deposit will be returned, but not otherwise.

[FOR A LARGE SHOW].

Class No.	APPLIANCES.	First Prize.	Second Prize.	Third Prize.
	A price must be affixed to each exhibit in Classes 511 to 513, the price named to include every portion of the exhibit staged.			
510	COLLECTION OF HIVES AND APPLIANCES, to include, among other articles, the following :— Three Frame-Hives complete, fitted with arrangements for Supering. A suitable OUTFIT FOR A BEGINNER in Bee-keeping (the Entries for which are to be grouped together and separate from the main exhibit). 1 pair of Section Racks fitted with sections; 1 Extractor; 1 slow stimulating Feeder; 1 rapid Feeder; 1 Smoker or other Instrument for quieting Bees; 1 Super Clearer; 1 Veil; 1 Swarm Box for travelling purposes; 1 Nucleus Hive for travelling; 1 Travelling Crate for Comb Honey. Class 510 is open only to Manufacturers of Bee Appliances, being articles sold in their usual way of trade, and as far as possible of the Exhibitor's own Manufacture. Staged by the Exhibitor or his representative on 50 superficial feet. Price to be affixed to each article. No articles must be added to the collection, nor any portion of the Exhibit removed, during the Show.	80/-	40/-	20/-
511	Best and most complete FRAME-HIVE, for general use, unpainted	20/-	15/-	10/-
512	Most complete and inexpensive FRAME-HIVE for Cottager's use, unpainted, price not to exceed 10/6	20/-	15/-	10/-
513	HONEY EXTRACTOR	15/-	10/-	Cert. of Merit.
514	OBSERVATORY HIVE, with not less than three Brood Frames with Bees and Queen; each comb to be visible on both sides. (*The hive must be provided with arrangements for the flight of the Bees during the time of the Show*).	20/-	15/-	10/-
515	ANY APPLIANCE connected with Bee-keeping, to which no Prize has been awarded at a Show of the Royal Agricultural Society of England. ...	10/-	Cert. of Merit.	Cert. of Merit.

HONEY.

516	Twelve Sections of COMB HONEY, of any year, approximate weight 12 lbs.	20/-	15/-	10/-

L 2

Class No.	HONEY.—Continued.	First Prize.	Second Prize.	Third Prize.
517	Twelve Jars of RUN or EXTRACTED LIGHT-COLOURED HONEY, of any year, gross weight to approximate 12 lbs. (*See Regulation* 6) ...	20/-	15/-	10/-
518	Twelve Jars of RUN or EXTRACTED MEDIUM or DARK-COLOURED HONEY, of any year, excluding Heather Honey, gross weight to approximate 12 lbs. (*See Regulation* 6)...	20/-	15/-	10/-
519	Twelve Jars of GRANULATED HONEY, of any year, gross weight to approximate 12 lbs.	20/-	15/-	10/-

MISCELLANEOUS, OPEN CLASSES.

520	Three Shallow-frames of COMB HONEY, for extracting, gathered during 1912 ...	20/-	15/-	10/-
521	Six Jars of HEATHER HONEY, of any year, gross weight to approximate 6 lbs. (*See Regulation* 6)	20/-	15/-	10/-
522	Six Jars of HEATHER-MIXTURE EXTRACTED HONEY, of any year, gross weight to approximate 6 lbs. ...	20/-	15/-	10/-
523	Best and most Attractive DISPLAY OF HONEY in any form, and of any year, staged on space 3 ft. by 3 ft., maximum height to be about 4 ft. above the table. The gross weight to be stated. *[The Exhibits in this class to be staged by the Exhibitors or their representatives.] *Regulation 6, *in regard to the size of the bottles or jars, does not apply to this Class, but Regulation* 5, *re lace edging, does apply.*	30/-	20/-	10/-
524	Exhibit of not less than 2 lbs. of WAX, the produce of the Exhibitor's Apiary; extracted and cleaned by the Exhibitor or his Assistants ...	10/-	7/6	5/-
525	Exhibit of not less than 3 lbs. of WAX, the produce of the Exhibitor's Apiary; extracted and cleaned by the Exhibitor or his Assistants. To be shewn in shape, quality and package suitable for the retail trade ...	10/-	7/6	5/-
526	HONEY VINEGAR, 1 quart, in clear glass bottles ...	7/6	5/-	Cert. of Merit.
527	MEAD, 1 quart, in clear glass bottles...	7/6	5/-	Cert. of Merit.
528	EXHIBIT of a Practical or Interesting Nature connected with Bee Culture, not mentioned in the foregoing Classes, including Candy for Bee Feeding, Articles of Food, or Medicine in which Honey is an ingredient ...	10/-	Cert. of Merit.	Cert. of Merit.
529	EXHIBIT of a Scientific Nature not mentioned in the foregoing Classes, to which no Prize has been awarded at a Show of the Royal Agricultural Society of England ...	10/-	Cert. of Merit.	Cert. of Merit.

BEE PRODUCE.

[FOR A SMALL SHOW].

Class.	1st Prize.	2nd Prize.	3rd Prize.
1—For the Best Hive suitable for Bee-keeping on the most approved modern system. Price not to exceed 20s. complete.	15/0	10/0	5/0
2—For the best display of Bee products (Honey, Wax, Mead, Vinegar, &c.), space not to exceed 3 ft. by 3ft.	20/0	10/0	7/6
3—For the best 12 1-lb. Sections of Honey. 1st Prize, Silver Medal of B.B.K.A. 2nd Prize, Bronze ditto. 3rd Prize, Certificate ditto.			
4—For the best 6 1-lb. Sections of Honey	10/0	7/6	5/0
5—For the best 12 1-lb. Jars of Extracted Honey	10/0	7/6	5/0
6—For the best 6 1-lb. Jars of Extracted Honey	10/0	7/6	5/0
7—For the best 6 1-lb. Jars of Granulated Honey	7/6	5/0	3/0
8—For the best Shallow Comb for Extracting	5/0	2/6	1/6
9—For the best Exhibit of this year's Wax not less than 1-lb.	5/0	2/6	1/6

ENTRY FEES.

2/- for First Entry, and 1/- each afterwards. Members of ——— are privileged to enter at half-fees.

Classes 1 and 2 are open to all. Classes 3, 4, 7, 8, and 9 open to all Members.

Class 6 is open only to Members who have never gained a first prize at the Annual Show.

———————————————— Bee-Keepers' Association.

Honey Show at ————————

AUGUST ————.

Class.	DESCRIPTION OF ENTRY. Only one entry on each line.	* Selling Price.			Entrance Fees.		
		TOTAL £					

I do hereby certify: That each and all the above particulars are correct to the best of my knowledge and belief.

I do hereby engage: (1) To prove the correctness of this Certificate to the satisfaction of the Committee or Judges, if called upon by them to do so.

I do hereby engage: (2) To conform, as an Exhibitor, to all the Rules and Regulations stated in the Prize List of the ————————— Bee-Keepers' Association.

Signature of Exhibitor..

Address.. *Date*......................

* Five per cent. commission will be charged on Honey sold.

All Entries, with Fees, to be sent to ————

on or before August ——.

Intending Exhibitors will greatly oblige by making their Entries early.

BEE PRODUCE. 151

RULES AND REGULATIONS.

For a Small Show.

1.—Every article must be the bona fide property of the Exhibitor.

2.—Exhibits of Honey must have been gathered from flowers by the Exhibitor's own bees, and, unless otherwise stated in the Schedule, must be the produce of the current year. Exhibits of Wax must have been obtained from the Exhibitor's own bees.

3.—Comb Honey must be glazed on both sides. The glass may be secured by metal clips or paper edging, which must be of such a width as to leave $3\frac{1}{2}$ inches by $3\frac{1}{2}$ inches of glass clear of paper edging, or in any other neat way capable of easy removal by the Judge. Sections or Frames of Comb Honey may be exhibited in single cases only.

4.—Run or extracted Honey must be exhibited in plain white glass jars, each containing 1 lb. nominal weight. The jars must not exceed six inches in height, and must be all the same shape in each exhibit.

5.—No Exhibitor shall be allowed to take more than one prize in any class, nor shall the joint owners of an apiary, or members of the same family, be allowed to make separate entries.

6.—The selling price of all Hives must be entered in the Certificate of Entry, and the Exhibitor must undertake to supply at the same price any number of similar Hives during the following twelve months.

7.—The Judge shall be empowered to withold prizes in case of insufficient merit.

8.—The show Committee reserve the right to decline any entry, to submit any exhibit for analysis, and to dispose of Honey which may have become damaged in transit or otherwise at any reasonable price, or to return the same at once to the Exhibitor. If any portion of a consignment of Honey or Wax sent for Exhibition is found to be adulterated, the whole exhibit and the Fees paid shall be forfeited.

9.—Every Exhibit and every detachable part of an exhibit must be legibly marked with the number provided by the Secretary of the Show. Packing cases should be similarly

BEE PRODUCE.

numbered. No card, label, trade mark, or name of exhibitor shall be placed on any exhibit until the conclusion of the judging. All Exhibits must be delivered, carriage paid, at the Show, not later than   o'clock a.m., and addressed to the Secretary. Numbers and address labels will be sent to each Exhibitor.

10.—Any protest against the decision of the Judge shall be made in writing and handed to the Secretary before 5 p.m. on the day of the Show. Such protests shall be heard and determined by the Executive of the Show, or may be referred by them to the Committee of the Association.

11.—Any question as to the true interpretation of the foregoing Rules shall be decided by the Committee of the Association.

CHAPTER XV.

Attractive and Educational Work.

The show should be made attractive and as educational as possible. It should be so arranged that a separate tent or building may be devoted to the exhibits, and that they are not mixed up with other departments.

The staging should be arranged so that visitors are allowed to pass in at one end and out at the other, in this way avoiding the blocking of the gangways, which would otherwise take place, and preventing the public from properly inspecting the exhibits. Non-competitive exhibits should be encouraged, as they are educational, fill out the show, and make it more imposing than it otherwise would be. Appliance manufacturers should also have every facility given for making a display, by providing them with space for their exhibits without charge. Although it is a good advertisement for them, such an exhibit entails a great deal of labour and expense. Fig. 57 gives a good idea of the value of these entries when nicely arranged in making a show attractive.

If it can be managed, several members of the show committee, each wearing a conspicuous badge, should always be about, from whom the public could obtain information. If there is no class for observatory hives, one marked " not for competition " should be staged, as such a hive is usually a great source of interest. Leaflets giving a description of bee-keeping, together with specimen copies of the *British Bee Journal* and the *Bee-Keepers' Record*, and reports of the local association, should be provided for giving away to those interested. These must not be distributed indiscriminately, but should be in the hands of those members of the committee who are present, so that they can give them where they will not be wasted. The Secretary should

BEE PRODUCE. 155

Fig. 58. The "Herrod" Demonstrating Tent, packed for Transit.

also have his receipt book with him for the enrolling of new members.

Lectures and demonstrations with live bees should also be given if possible, as this furthers the work of the Association to a considerable extent. There are some who object to these from a selfish motive, stating that they induce too many people to take up bee-keeping, and in this way tend to lower the price of honey. This is foolish reasoning, because there is ample room for hundreds of more bee-keepers in the country, and honey of good quality properly prepared will always fetch a fair price.

I have numerous proofs that bee-tent lectures have been the means of inducing many persons to take up bee-keeping. Some of them are leading men in the craft to-day, not only in this country, but also abroad. There are hundreds of people who in the winter would never think of going to a lecture on bees in a room, but at a show the crowd around

156 PRODUCING, PREPARING, EXHIBITING

the tent often attracts them; they listen to what is being said, and, becoming interested, often take to bee-keeping. I would like to emphasise one point, which is that the lecturer should be careful in his remarks and not lead his audience to believe, as so often is the case, that bee-keeping is an Eldorado, or that money can be made from bees without trouble. He should make it quite plain that only those prepared to carry out the work properly, and who will not be daunted by failures in bad

Fig. 59. The "Herrod" Demonstrating Tent in Use.

seasons, should take up bee-keeping. All statements with regard to abnormal takes, should be carefully avoided, and an average return, rather under than over, should be quoted, otherwise the daily papers get hold of such statements and magnify them, thus tending to lower the prices of home produce.

The demonstrating tent must not be too far away from the honey department, and should be made as prominent as possible. The present-day tent is very different from the old style, which was a cart-load in itself. My own tent can go as passengers' luggage, for it packs up very neatly, as may be seen in Fig. 58, and can be carried easily by one man, fixed in ten minutes, and taken down in five. There is no centre pole to obstruct the view of the audience, or an obstacle in the way of the lecturer, and there is no ironwork about it at all. Six light bamboo poles, with the same number of stakes and ropes, constitute all the support it requires. It is seen in use in Fig. 59, and has been used for the past four years at the Royal Show, where the largest crowds congregate at demonstrations in this country.

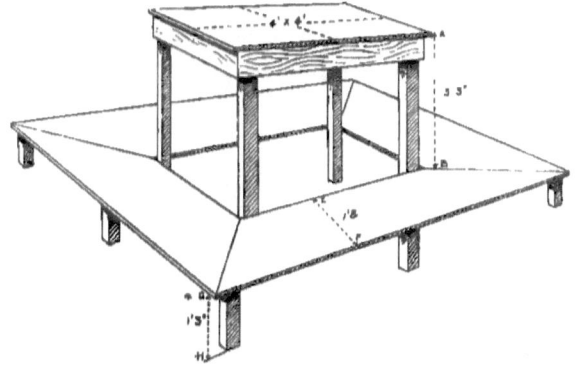

Fig. 61. A Lecturer's Demonstrating Table.

It is sixteen feet in diameter and eight feet high, and will do equally well for small shows. If compared with that in Fig. 60 a great difference will be seen. The net curtain is all that is necessary, for the verandah and outside canvas curtain of old days were only of use for preventing those from seeing the demonstrations who did not pay for going inside. No charge is ever made now, so these parts are useless. One or two other points long experience in this kind of work has taught me are essential for success. A good demonstrating table is necessary, and the one I have found most useful is illustrated in Fig. 61, showing the measurements of each part. Such a table gives free-

dom in working, and enables the audience, even in the back rows, to see all that is going on upon it. If possible, the tent should be placed in the shade of trees. Talking and demonstrating at the same time is very fatiguing work, and if the sun beats down upon the operator, this, with the heat which rises from the bees, is almost unbearable, and I have a vivid recollection of being on the point of collapsing on several occasions when placed in such a position. The lectures should not last too long, otherwise people will not stay to hear them to the end, as there are other attractions at such shows. Half an hour for each lecture is quite sufficient. They should not be too advanced, but purely elementary, with a view to interesting the man in the street. Explanations are rendered more clear if a fully fitted frame hive, without bees, is used for illustration. I have been at shows where it has been insisted that at each lecture a particular branch of bee-keeping should be described. At such, people stand and listen for a minute or two, and, as they cannot understand what is being said, yawn, and pass on. Those who already know a little about bee-keeping can always learn more by asking questions after the lecture. Both the skep and movable comb systems of bee-keeping should be shown, explained, and compared. Many bee-keepers object to driving being shown, and maintain that it is now out of date and useless. To a certain extent this is true, but there is no doubt that the driving of bees attracts an audience, even if it serves no other purpose, and when people once stop to see what is going on, it remains for the lecturer to keep their attention. There are still many skeps kept in the country, a fact proved by the number of driven bees which are advertised. Recently I saw over one hundred such in one apiary, and less than a couple of years ago I was present at a show not sixty miles from London where the only honey shown was in old-fashioned straw caps from skeps. A difficulty with regard to skeps is in their being generally too full of honey to take to shows, and in hot weather the combs often break down. I gave up

160   PRODUCING, PREPARING, EXHIBITING

some years ago borrowing skeps of bees for demonstrating purposes from bee-keepers in the neighbourhood, because very few know what is required for this purpose, and the skeps would arrive with all the combs broken, because they had not been secured by skewers, or the bees had been suffocated by being tied up with both stand and hive in a sack. Skeps about half full of comb were also sometimes

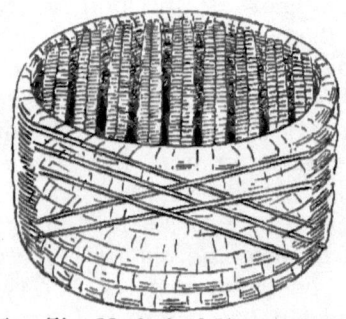

Fig. 62. The Method of Skewering Combs.

brought, while not infrequently they were overflowing with bees, and it was only on rare occasions that suitable material to work with was obtained. Now my practice is to take my own bees, both in skeps and movable comb hives. Only those skeps having good, old, tough combs should be used, and these should be well secured by means of five skewers, as shown in Fig. 62. Three put in from one side and two from the other. The skewers should be made of deal half an inch square, and pushed through in a slanting direction from the bottom to the top, by which means they are interlocked and cannot move. The combs should not be too full of stores, nor the bees too numerous, about a quart of them being ample, and a skep can be very easily kept in this condition by the experienced bee-keeper. The travelling crate used for carrying a skep of bees is shown in Fig. 63. It is complete, and can be unfastened or fastened in a few seconds by means of universal fasteners, shown at the top.

Plenty of room is allowed between the top cross-pieces and the scrim cloth to allow the smoker, which is a specially made miniature one, to be strapped on, as shown in illustration, and there is also plenty of ventilation provided for it when in the parcels van of a train, as the top cross-pieces prevent parcels from coming in contact with the scrim cloth. The driving irons are strapped on one side with the points

Fig. 63. The "Herrod" Skep Carrier for Demonstration Purposes.

protected by means of blocks of wood. Holes in the top block allow for the storage of about three two-and-a-half inch round wire nails to act as skewers. Before putting on the scrim a cross-piece of wood, made of deal, three-quarters of an inch square, is laid over the combs, thus providing a space between them and the scrim for the bees to cluster in. A piece of corrugated paper for smoker fuel placed under the skep makes the outfit complete.

162 PRODUCING, PREPARING, EXHIBITING

The box used for bees on movable combs is shown in Fig. 64. It holds five frames, the bottom being made of perforated zinc, and a large square hole, covered with the same material, is left in the lid, which fastens with universal fasteners, the entrance being covered with a hinged perforated door.

The lecturer's kit, fitted up in this manner, packs into a very small compass, as shown in Fig. 65, which illustrates tent, bees, and other necessaries, loaded on a small motor-car.

Fig. 64. A Travelling Box for Demonstration of Bees on Movable Combs.

On arrival at the show-ground the first thing to do is to liberate the bees. They should never be allowed to fly in the tent, or they will become a nuisance to the operator, as also to the audience, and it often results in the latter getting stung.

A shady place under a hedge or trees should be found for them some little distance from the tent, and away from all traffic. If they have a couple of hours' flight before being brought into the tent they will mark the position, and when they fly up during the demonstration will go straight to this location, and thus avoid giving trouble in or round the bee tent.

The manipulator should not wear a veil, for this gives a false impression as to the temper of bees, but he should point out how necessary a veil is as a precaution when bees are on the stands they have always occupied. Foolish exhibitions, such as putting bees in a hat, and placing this on the head, should be avoided, as it gives the impression that it is a bee-taming exhibition, instead of an educational one. The general public have too much of this idea already, for they often inquire, " What time is the performance to

Fig. 65. Lecturer's Kit Packed on Small Motor-car.

take place?" To demonstrate their harmlessness when properly handled, all that is necessary is to take a handful of bees, and if possible show that there is nothing unusual in it, and that other people can do likewise. Try and get one of the audience to imitate what has been done.

A glass-topped box, in which to show the queen, should be provided, care being taken to ask that when it is going round for viewing, the sun should not be allowed to shine

Indoor Demonstration by the Author, Grocers' Exhibition at the Agricultural Hall, London.

Fig. 66. Indoor Demonstration Department, Grocers' Exhibition at the Agricultural Hall, London.

into it. I have lost several good queens from this not being done.

The leaflets on "How to Keep Bees," supplied gratuitously by the B.B.K.A., for giving away, are also most useful.

Demonstrations can well be carried out indoors. The author was the first to institute indoor demonstrations during the autumn at large London shows. Fig. 66 shows the demonstration stall and tent at the Grocers' Exhibition, held in the Royal Agricultural Hall, Islington. The work can be carried out even by electric light without loss of bees. If the hive is stood on a shelf placed near the top of the tent the bees find their way back to it between the demonstrations. The tent used is a small one, so that if the bees creep along instead of flying they are able to find their way home. Four daily demonstrations were carried out for seven days without the loss of more than a score of bees.

THE SLAUGHTER OF THE DRONES.

INDEX.

	PAGE
Appliances, choice of, for show	115, 116
Amateur	121
Arrangements of show	153
Bee candy	104
Bees, strain of, for comb honey	67
Foreign unsuitable	67
Bell glasses	43, 80, 81
Kind to use	80
Obtaining straight combs in	80, 81
Cakes	45, 46
Preparation of	93
Recipes for	93, 95
Classes for single jars or sections	81, 82
Sale	82
Comb honey, to liquefy when granulated	61, 62
Cappings of	70
Colour of	71
Designs	81
Grading sections	71
Producing and preparing	67
Confectionery, recipes for	96-98
Bee candy	104
Recipe for bee candy	104
Demonstrations	155
Box for queen	163, 166
Form of tent	156, 157
Indoor	166
Literature for	153, 166
Packing crate for skep	160, 161
Position of tent for	156
Size of tent	157
Skeps for	160, 161
Skewering combs in skep	160
Table for	157, 159
Travelling box for movable combs	162
Where to place bees for	162, 163
Dividers for section racks	69
For shallow combs	79
Entry form	150
Exhibiting, advantages of	22, 23
Inducements for	26, 27, 30, 32
Not a monopoly	32
Private	23, 24
Exhibitors	9-11
Advice to	19
Mistakes of	19, 22

	PAGE
Exhibits, supervision of	16
Addressing	136
Advice of awards	136, 137
Amateur appliances	121
Damage to	16
Despatching	136
Educational	120, 121
Inventions	119, 120
Non-competitive	153
Packing	122-128, 130-132, 134
Railway carriage	135
Railway note for	138-140
Scientific	120
Staging	16
Extractors	118, 119
Grading honey glasses	19
Grading	59, 60
Granulated honey, kinds to show	64
Preparation of	62, 64
Heather blend, preparation of	66
Heather, to press	65
Kind to choose for show	66
Storage of	65
Hives, points in judging	49
Material for	49
The kind to show	115, 116
Honey medicines, recipes for	98-101
Honey, Reid honey taster	38, 42
As an article of food for infants	101, 103, 104
Cleanliness	55
Grading	59, 60
Granulated	62
Heather	64-66
Heather blend	66
Heating	57-59, 61
Improving	57-59
Jars for	55, 56
Kinds to show	62, 64, 66
Means of disposing of	141, 143
Producing and preparing extracted	55-66
Putting in jars	57, 64
Straining	57
Jars, shape of, for show	55
Preparation of	56, 57
Judges	5, 7-9
Badges for	15, 16
Book for	12
Entrance ticket for	15
Water, biscuits, or apples for	15

INDEX.

	PAGE
Judging points of liquid	34, 36
Comparative method	54
Fallacy of set points	50-52, 54
Granulated	37
Heather	37, 38
Heather blend	38
Hives and Appliances	49
Observatory hives	46, 47
Sections	39, 42
Trophies	47, 48
Lectures, use of	155
Form of	156, 159
Length of time of	159
Mead	45, 91, 92
Recipe for	93
Observatory hives, points of	46, 47
Kind to use	105-107
Packing	122
Box for extracted	123
Cardboard cases for	123
Hives	130
Non-returnable box for	126, 127
Not to wrap jars	123, 124
Post	132
Separate boxes for each exhibit	131
Single jars and sections	132, 134
Spring crate for sections	125, 130
To fasten box	125
Wax	130
Wrong box	123
Wrong method	128
Rules and regulations,	144-146, 151, 152
Schedules	147-149
Secretaries, instructions for	11, 12, 14-18
Receipt book	153, 155
Sections, faking	42
Bleaching	78
Cardboard boxes for	77
Cleaning	73
Colour of cappings	71
Glazing	73, 74

	PAGE
Sections (contd.).	
Glazing machine	74, 76
Grading	71
Grannlated	42, 43
Judging	39, 42
Kind of cells	71
Kind to use	67, 68
Method of obtaining from swarm	69, 70
Not the way to Stage	77
Over-lacing	43, 74
Racks	68, 69
Removal of	70
Syrup fed	43
Template for	43
To liquefy when granulated	61, 62
To prepare	68
Shallow combs	43
Cases for	78
Kind of cells	78
Stewards, duties of	18
Thermometer, use of	61
Trophies, points of	47, 48
Cakes, wax, and bye-products for	111
How to build	107, 108, 110, 111
Shop window displays	113, 115
Use of flowers on	111
Vinegar	45, 91
Recipe for	91
Wax, colour of	43, 87
Boxes for	87
Cases for retail classes	90
Choice of	83
Floor polish	104
For retail classes	88-90
Giving aroma to	87
Moulding	84-87
Moulding for retail classes	89
Scales for	15
Testing	44
Weston extractor	83

www.ingramcontent.com/pod-product-compliance
Lightning Source LLC
Chambersburg PA
CBHW020356170426
43200CB00005B/188